THE
POWER
—— OF ——
YOU

Other Books by John Mason

Believe You Can—
The Power of a Positive Attitude

Be Yourself—
Discover the Life You Were Meant to Live

Never Give Up—
You're Stronger Than You Think

Proverbs Prayers

Seize Today

You Can Be Your Best—Starting Today

You Can Do It—Even if Others Say You Can't

THE
POWER
— OF —
YOU

INSPIRATION FOR
BEING **YOUR BEST SELF**

John Mason

Revell
a division of Baker Publishing Group
Grand Rapids, Michigan

© 2003, 2011, 2012 by John Mason

Published by Revell
a division of Baker Publishing Group
PO Box 6287, Grand Rapids, MI 49516-6287
www.revellbooks.com

Repackaged edition published 2021
ISBN 978-0-8007-3957-7
eISBN 978-1-4934-2889-2

Taken from material previously published in three separate volumes:
The Impossible Is Possible © 2003
You're Born an Original—Don't Die a Copy © 2011
Let Go of Whatever Holds You Back © 2012

Printed in the United States of America

21 22 23 24 25 26 27   7 6 5 4 3 2 1

Contents

Contents

PART 2: LOOKING OUTWARD

Contents

PART 3: LOOKING UPWARD

Contents

— Part One —

LOOKING

INWARD

Passion Is the
Spark for Your Fuse

God put inside every person the potential to be passionate. One person with passion makes a greater impact than the passive force of ninety-nine who have only interest. Too many people have "only interest" in their destiny. The book of Ecclesiastes says, "Whatsoever thy hand findeth to do, do it with thy might" (9:10). The atmosphere of your life changes dramatically when you add enthusiasm.

Everyone loves something. We're shaped and motivated by what we love. Ignore what you are passionate about and you ignore one of the greatest potentials God has put inside you. What gets your heart racing? What are you hungry to learn and know more about? What do you daydream about doing? What captures your heart and your attention?

My friend Neil Eskelin shares the following story from his outstanding book *Yes Yes Living in a No No World*:

> I was attending an awards banquet of the Chase National Life Insurance Company. The speaker was the famed author of *Think and Grow Rich*, Napoleon Hill.
>
> When Hill was introduced it was obvious his age had caught up with him. We all wondered if the octogenarian would be physically able to give the speech. (He passed away not long after this event.)
>
> Napoleon Hill slowly walked to the podium, placed both of his hands on the sides of it, looked out at the audience and announced, "Ladies and gentlemen, I have given this speech hundreds and hundreds of times in my life. But tonight I am going to deliver it the best it has ever been given. This is going to be the best speech of my life!"

Wow! It was like a bolt of lightning. I watched 300 adults move to the edge of their chairs and absorb every word like a sponge.

Enthusiasm always makes others stand up and take notice. Nothing significant was ever achieved without enthusiasm. Jesus was a passionate man. He died for us because He loved His Father and us passionately.

Most winners are just ex-losers who got passionate. The worst bankruptcy in the world is the person who has lost his enthusiasm. When you add passion and emotion to belief, it becomes a conviction. There's a big difference between a belief and a conviction. Belief agrees with the facts. Conviction brings persistent action to your belief.

Driven by passionate conviction, you can do anything you want with your life—except give up on something you care about. Mike Murdock says, "What generates passion and zeal in you is a clue to revealing your destiny. What you love is a clue to something you contain."

Fulfilling God's plan is a passionate idea or it is nothing. There's a reason we're told to "serve the LORD thy God with all thy heart and with all thy soul" (Deut. 10:12). Henri Frederic Ameil reminds us, "Without passion man is a mere latent force and a possibility, like the flint which awaits the shock of the iron before it can give forth its spark."

You must first be a believer, then an achiever. "There are many things that will catch my eye, but there are only a very few that catch my heart . . . it is those I consider to pursue" (Tim Redmond).

The Person with Imagination Is Never Alone and Never Finished

Christians should be viewed not as empty bottles to be filled, but as candles to be lit. You were built for creativity. Your eyes look for opportunity, your ears listen for direction, your mind requires a challenge, and your heart longs for God's way. Your heart has eyes that the brain knows nothing of.

Make a daily demand on your creativity. Everything starts as somebody's daydream. All people of action are first dreamers. The wonder of imagination is this: it has the power to light its own fire. Ability is a flame, creativity is a fire. Originality sees things with a fresh vision. Unlike an airplane, your imagination can take off day or night in any kind of weather or circumstances. So let it fly!

First Corinthians 2:16 says, "We have the mind of Christ." Don't you know we've been given His creativity too?

A genius is someone who shoots at something no one else sees and hits it. We are told never to cross a bridge till we come to it, but this world is owned by those who have "crossed bridges" in their imaginations far ahead of the crowd. Our challenge is to consider the future and act before it occurs.

Many times we act, or fail to act, not because of will, as is so commonly believed, but because of imagination. Your dreams are an indicator of your potential greatness.

Grandmother saw Billy running around the house slapping himself and asked him why. "Well," said Billy, "I just got so tired of walking I thought I'd ride my horse for a while." One day Michelangelo saw a block of marble that the owner said was of no value. "It is valuable to me," said Michelangelo. "There is an angel imprisoned in it and I must set it free."

Other people may be smarter, better educated, or more experienced than you, but no single person has a corner on dreams, desire, or ambition. The creation of a thousand forests of opportunity can spring forth from one small acorn of an idea. As Woodrow Wilson once said, "No man that does not see visions will ever realize any high hope or undertake any high enterprise."

The Bible says, "Where there is no vision, the people perish" (Prov. 29:18). That's not God's best for you. Dissatisfaction and discouragement result not from the absence of things but from the absence of vision. Not being a person of imagination causes your life to be less than it was intended to be.

A dream is the most exciting thing there is.

Don't Build a Case against Yourself

What does God think about your future? We find the answer in Jeremiah 29:11, which says, "'I know the plans I have for you,' declares the LORD, 'plans to prosper you and not to harm you, plans to give you hope and a future'" (NIV). All of what we are, both good and bad, is what we have thought and believed. What you've become is the price you paid to get what you used to want.

All of the important battles we face will be waged within ourselves. Nothing great has ever been achieved except by those who dared to believe that God inside of them was superior to any circumstance. First John 4:4 says, "Greater is he that is in you, than he that is in the world."

Building a case against yourself presents thousands of reasons why you can't do what you want to, when all you really need is one reason why you can. It's a great deal better to *do* all the things you should than to spend the rest of your life wishing you had. It's been said, "Don't put water in your own boat; the storm will put enough in on its own." The first key victory you must win is over yourself. Your chief competition is *you*.

> You can't consistently perform in a manner inconsistent with the way you see yourself.
>
> Zig Ziglar

Amazingly, sometimes what you think is your greatest weakness can become a wonderful strength. Take, for example, the story of one ten-year-old boy who decided to study judo despite the fact that he had lost his left arm in a devastating car accident.

The boy began lessons with an old Japanese judo master. He was doing well, so he couldn't understand why, after three months of training, the master had taught him only one move.

"Sensei," the boy finally said, "shouldn't I be learning more moves?"

"This is the only move you know, but this is the only move you'll ever need to know," his master replied.

Not quite understanding but believing in his teacher, the boy kept training.

Several months later, the master took the boy to his first tournament.

Surprising himself, the boy easily won his first two matches. The third match proved to be more difficult, but after some time, his opponent became impatient and charged; the boy deftly used his one move to win the match.

Still amazed by his success, the boy was now in the finals.

This time, his opponent was bigger, stronger, and more experienced. For a while, the boy appeared to be overmatched. Concerned that the boy might get hurt, the referee called a timeout. He was about to stop the match when the sensei intervened.

"No," the sensei insisted. "Let him continue."

Soon after the match resumed, the boy's opponent made a critical mistake and dropped his guard. Instantly, the boy used his move to pin him. The boy had won the match and the tournament. He was the champion.

On the way home, the boy and his sensei reviewed every move from each and every match. Then the boy summoned the courage to ask what was really on his mind.

"Sensei, how did I win the tournament with only one move?"

"You won for two reasons," the teacher answered. "First, you've almost mastered one of the most difficult throws in all of judo. And second, the only known defense for that move is for your opponent to grab your left arm."

The boy's biggest weakness had become his biggest strength.

The great evangelist Dwight L. Moody said, "I've never met a man who gave me as much trouble as myself." Yes, we all relate to that. Follow the advice of my good friend Dave Blunt: "Stay out of your own way!"

Building a case against yourself is like a microscope—it magnifies trifling things but can't receive great ones. Here's a little formula to keep from building a case against yourself: multiply your prayer time, divide the truth from a lie, subtract negative influences, and add God's Word. We lie loudest when we lie to ourselves. Both faith and fear sail into the harbor of your mind, but allow only faith to drop anchor.

Dismiss all the cases you've made against yourself.

Go Out on a Limb—
That's Where the
Fruit Is

Be bold and courageous. When you look back on your life, you'll regret the things you didn't do more than the things you did. When facing a difficult task, act as though it is impossible to fail. If you're going to climb Mount Everest, bring along the American flag. Go from looking at what you can see to believing what you can have. Don't undertake a plan unless it is distinctly important and nearly impossible. Don't bunt—aim out of the ballpark. The only limits are, as always, those of vision.

Security is mostly a stranger. It doesn't exist in nature, nor do the children of men experience it. Avoiding danger is no safer in the long run than outright exposure. Life is either a daring adventure or nothing.

Helen Keller

Mediocre people don't think of themselves as mediocre. William Winans says, "Not doing more than the average is what keeps the average down." And Ronald Osborn challenges, "Undertake something that's difficult; it will do you good. Unless you try to do something beyond what you have already mastered, you will never grow." It's difficult to say what is truly impossible, for what we take for granted today was seemingly impossible yesterday. "Impossible," Napoleon is quoted as saying, "is a word found only in the dictionary of fools." What words are found in your dictionary?

One who is afraid of doing too much always does too little. To achieve all that's possible, we must attempt the impossible. The impossible is possible! Your vision becomes your potential worth. Learn to be comfortable with great dreams.

The best jobs haven't been found. The best work hasn't been done. Christians must not stay in the shadows but stretch in the light of the cross. A person who expects nothing will never be disappointed. The only way to discover the limits of the natural is to go beyond them into the supernatural. Ask yourself, "Is anything too hard for the LORD?" (Gen. 18:14).

The readiness to take risks is our grasp of faith. William Lloyd George said, "Don't be afraid to take a big step if one is indicated; you can't cross a chasm in two small jumps." God puts no restriction on faith; faith puts no restriction on God. "But without faith it is impossible to please him" (Heb. 11:6). Your vision must be bigger than you. You should say with the psalmist, "Lead me to the rock that is higher than I" (Ps. 61:2).

"Don't avoid extremes to stay 'in balance,' stay in balance by living in the extreme God wills at that time in your life" (Tim Redmond). Unless a man takes on more than he possibly can do, he will never do all he can. Charles

Spurgeon motivated his listeners by saying, "Brethren, be great believers. Little faith will bring your souls to heaven, but great faith will bring heaven to your souls."

The most disappointed people in the world are those who get just what is coming to them and no more. There are a lot of ways to become a failure, but never taking a chance is the most successful. Some things have to be believed to be seen. Attempt something so fantastic that unless God is in it it's destined for failure.

Don't bother with small plans; they motivate no one. Nothing significant was ever accomplished by a realistic person.

Invest in Yourself

God regularly sends us divine opportunities for investment in ourselves. Be on the lookout for them. He does this first through His Word, which is the best investment we can put into ourselves. But He also sends many other "investment opportunities" to us. In my own life, I've incorporated many of these. For example, my wife and I have a weekly date night that has been a great investment in our marriage. Also, every Saturday when the kids were little we would "sneak out" on Mom to have an early breakfast together. This time was great for the kids and me, while allowing my wife a nice quiet break.

Everything you say or do creates an investment somewhere. Whether that investment generates a dividend or a loss depends on you. Always do your best, for what you plant now you will harvest later.

One of the biggest mistakes you can make is to believe you work for someone else. No matter how many bosses you appear to have, you really work for the Lord. You can't look to others as your source. That's why tapping into God's investment opportunities is so important. They are His way of developing and instructing us. When an archer misses the mark, he turns and looks for the fault within himself. Failure to hit the bull's-eye is never the fault of the target. "To improve your aim—improve yourself" (Gilbert Arland).

When prosperity comes, don't spend it all; give some back to others and make an investment in yourself. Half of knowing what you want is knowing what you must give up before you get it. Time invested in improving ourselves cuts down on time wasted in disapproving others.

"Study to [show] thyself approved unto God,

a workman that needeth not to be ashamed" (2 Tim. 2:15). Investment doesn't cost, it pays. You cannot fulfill your destiny without applying the principle of investing in yourself.

People Say They Want Riches When What They Need Is Fulfillment of a Purpose

The world makes room for a person of purpose. Her words and actions demonstrate she *knows* where she's going. You're built to conquer circumstances, solve problems, and attain goals. You'll find no real satisfaction or happiness in life without obstacles to conquer, goals to achieve, and a purpose to accomplish. People may say they want money; what they really need is satisfaction. Happiness comes when you squander yourself for a purpose.

In your heart is a sleeping lion. No person alive can completely shun his or her destiny. Be on a mission. Have a definite sense of direction and purpose for your life. Successful lives are motivated by dynamic purpose. God can only bless your plan and direct you in accomplishing it if you have one. Strong convictions precede great actions.

As soon as you resign yourself to fate, your resignation is promptly accepted. You don't have a fate, you have a destiny. When you look into the future, it's so bright it will make you squint. "It's never too late to be what you might have been" (George Eliot).

"More men fail through lack of purpose than lack of talent" (Billy Sunday). If your method is hit or miss, you'll usually miss. "If you're not sure where you are going, you'll probably end up someplace else" (Robert F. Mager). Too many people don't know where they're going, but they're on their way. Growth for the sake of growth is the ideology of the cancer cell. Go forward with purpose.

The only thing some people do is grow older.

Ed Howe

Lord Chesterfield wrote, "Firmness of purpose is one of the most necessary sinews of character and one of the best instruments of success. Without it, genius wastes its efforts in a maze of inconsistencies." The man who has no direction is the slave of his circumstances. The poorest man is not he who is without a cent but he who is without a purpose. There's good news for each of us in walking out our purpose. Jesus said, "My yoke is easy, and my burden is light" (Matt. 11:30).

"If you don't have a vision for your life, then you probably haven't focused in on anything" (Dr. David Burns). In the absence of vision there can be no clear and constant focus. When your purpose is clear, decisions become more obvious. "When you discover your mission, you will feel its demand. It will fill you with enthusiasm and a burning desire to get to work on it" (W. Clement Stone).

If You're Not Failing,
You're Not Growing

An inspirational speaker began his seminar by holding up a twenty-dollar bill. He asked the two hundred people in the room, "Who would like this twenty-dollar bill?"

Hands started going up.

"I am going to give this twenty dollars to one of you," he said. "But first, let me do this," and he proceeded to crumple the bill.

He then asked, "Who still wants it?"

Still the hands were in the air.

"Well," he continued, "what if I do this?" And he dropped it on the ground and started to grind it into the floor with his shoe.

He picked it up, now all crumpled and dirty. "Now who still wants it?" Still the hands went into the air.

"My friends, you have all learned a very valuable lesson. No matter what I did to the money, you still wanted it because it did not decrease in value. It was still worth twenty dollars."

Many times in our lives, we are dropped, crumpled, and ground into the dirt by the decisions we make and the circumstances that come our way. We feel as though we are worthless. But no matter what has happened or what will happen, you will never lose your value.

We all make mistakes—especially those who do things. Failure is often the first necessary step toward success. If we don't take the risk of failing, we won't get the chance to succeed. When we're trying, we're winning. To fail is the natural consequence of trying. Babe Ruth, one of the great home run hitters but also the all-time strikeout leader, always said, "Never let the fear of striking out get in your way."

Stop trying to be perfect. When you have a serious decision to make, tell yourself firmly you are going to make it. Don't expect it will be a perfect one. I love the wisdom of Winston

Churchill: "The maxim 'nothing avails but perfection' may be spelled P-A-R-A-L-Y-S-I-S." The pursuit of excellence is gratifying and healthy; the pursuit of perfection is frustrating, neurotic, and a terrible waste of time.

> I don't like these cold, precise, perfect people who, in order not to speak wrong, never speak at all, and in order not to do wrong, never do anything.
>
> Henry Ward Beecher

The fact is, you're like a tea bag. You won't know your own strength until you've been through some hot water. Failure is something we can avoid only by saying nothing, doing nothing, and being nothing. "Remember, there are two benefits of failure. First, if you do fail, you learn what doesn't work; and second, the failure gives you an opportunity to try a new approach" (Roger Von Oech).

Some defeats are only installments to victory. "Even a mistake may turn out to be the one thing necessary to a worthwhile achievement"

(Henry Ford). Some people learn from their mistakes; some never recover from them. Learn how to fail intelligently. Develop success from failure.

Mistakes and failure are two of the surest stepping-stones to success. No other element can do so much for a person who is willing to study them and to make the most out of them. "Most people think of success and failure as opposites, but they are actually both products of the same process" (Roger Von Oech). Your season of failure is the best time for sowing your seeds of success.

Successful people are not afraid to fail. They go from failure to failure . . . until at last success is theirs. The best way to accelerate your success is to double your failure rate. The law of failure is one of the most powerful of all success laws.

No matter what mistakes you have made—no matter how you've messed things up—you can still make a new beginning. The person who fully realizes this suffers less from the shock and pain of failure and sooner gets off to a new beginning.

Norman Vincent Peale

"When you stumble today, pick yourself up tomorrow. That's what tomorrows are for" (Janet Collins). Often just before the big success . . . comes apparent failure and discouragement. "I hope someday to have so much of what the world calls success, that people will ask me, 'What's your secret?' And I will tell them, 'I just get up again when I fall down'" (Paul Harvey).

The greatest mistake you can make in life is to continually fear you will make one. "Don't be afraid to fail. Don't waste energy trying to cover up failure. If you're not failing, you're not growing" (H. Stanley Judd). When successful people stop growing and learning, it's usually because they have become less and less willing to risk failure. "Failure should be our teacher, not our undertaker. Failure is delay, not defeat. It is a temporary detour, not a dead-end street" (William A. Ward).

If you are made of the right stuff, a hard fall results in a sky-high bounce. A life spent making mistakes is not only more honorable but also more useful than a life spent doing nothing.

Get Ahead during the Time Others Waste

D on't be a person who says, "Ready. Aim
... aim ... aim ... aim ..." As fast as
each opportunity presents itself, use it! No matter how small an opportunity may be, use it!
Do the thing you have to do when it ought to
be done whether you like it or not. "He who
hesitates misses the green light, gets bumped in
the rear, and loses his parking space" (Herbert
Prochnow).

One of the deceptions of an unproductive
life is that this present day is not important.
Every day comes bearing its own gifts. Untie
the ribbons, tear into the wrapping, and open
them up. Write it on your heart: *every day is
the best day of the year.* "This is the day that

41

the LORD has made; let us rejoice and be glad in it" (Ps. 118:24 NRSV).

By the time the fool has learned to play the game, the players have dispersed and the rules have changed. Don't find yourself striking when the iron is cold. Instead, scratch opportunity where it itches. "Walk while ye have the light, lest darkness come upon you" (John 12:35). Life is made of constant calls to action.

"Successful leaders have the courage to take action while others hesitate" (John Maxwell). You never know what you can do until you try. Remember, the moment you say, "I give up," someone else is seeing the same situation and saying, "My, what a great opportunity." The fact is that no opportunity is ever lost; someone else just picks up the ones you missed. A secret of success in life is to be ready for opportunity when it comes. Ability is nothing without opportunity.

Time flies. It's up to you to be the pilot. "Everything comes to him who hustles while he waits" (Thomas Edison). It's been my observation that most successful people get ahead during the time others waste. A secret of success is to do something else in the meantime. Make quick use of the moment.

It is later than you think. Be ready now. God's alarm clock has no snooze button. It doesn't do any good to stand up and take notice if you sit down as soon as opportunity passes by. Look at it . . . size it up . . . make a decision. You postpone your life when you can't make up your mind. "If you wait for perfect conditions, you will never get anything done. . . . Keep on sowing your seed, for you never know which will grow—perhaps it all will" (Eccles. 11:4, 6 TLB).

William Ward has this recipe for success: "Study while others are sleeping; work while others are loafing; prepare while others are playing; and dream while others are wishing." There is no time like the present and no present like time. Those who take advantage of their advantage get the advantage in this world. Don't find yourself at the end of your life saying, "What a wonderful life I've had! I only wish I had realized and appreciated it sooner."

What You See
Depends Mainly on
What You Look For

The reason many people don't get answers
from God is the same reason a thief doesn't
find a policeman: they are running away. How
we position ourselves in life makes all the difference. To one person the world is desolate,
dull, and empty. To another the same world
looks rich, interesting, and full of meaning. The
choice is up to you. It's like how a twenty-dollar
bill looks so big when it goes to church and so
little when it goes out for groceries.

If you look at life the wrong way, there's always cause for alarm. Most people complain
because roses have thorns. Instead, be thankful

thorns have roses. What you see depends mainly on what you look for.

A young man was getting ready to graduate from college. For many months he had admired a beautiful sports car in a dealer's showroom. Knowing his father could well afford it, he told him that was all he wanted.

As graduation day approached, the young man awaited signs that his father had purchased the car. Finally, on the morning of his graduation, his father called him into his private study. His father told him how proud he was to have such a fine son and how much he loved him. He handed his son a beautifully wrapped gift box. Curious but somewhat disappointed, the young man opened the box and found a lovely, leather-bound Bible. Angrily, he raised his voice at his father and said, "With all your money you give me a Bible?" and stormed out of the house, leaving the holy book.

Many years passed and the young man was very successful in business. He had a beautiful home and a wonderful family. But he realized his father was now very old and thought perhaps he should go to him. He had not seen him since that graduation day. Before he could make arrangements, the man received a telegram telling him his father had passed away and willed all of his possessions to him. He needed to come home immediately and take care of things. When he arrived at his father's house, sudden sadness and regret filled his heart.

He began to search his father's important papers and saw the still-new Bible, just as he had left it years ago. Through tears, he opened the Bible and began to turn the pages. As he read those words, a car key dropped from an envelope taped behind the Bible. It had a tag with a dealer's name, the same dealer who had the sports car he had desired. On the tag was the date of his graduation and the words PAID IN FULL.

How many times do we miss God's blessings because they are not packaged as we expected?

Position yourself to *receive*, not *resist*. How you see things on the outside depends on how things are on the inside of you. "Any fact facing us is not as important as our attitude toward it, for that determines our success or failure" (Norman Vincent Peale). "You and I do not see things as they are. We see things as we are" (Herb Cohen). Develop the hunter's approach, the outlook that wherever you go there are ideas waiting to be discovered. When you are positioned right, opportunity presents itself.

Opportunity can be missed if you're broadcasting when you should be tuning in. When opportunity knocks, some people object to the interruption. "One of the greatest and most comforting truths is that when one door opens, another closes, but often we look so long and regretfully upon the closed door that we do not see the one that is open for us" (Anonymous).

See success where others see only failure. Expect something good to happen. That expectation will energize your dreams and give them momentum. You'll often find life responds to your outlook. We go where our vision is. Life is mostly a matter of expectation.

You'll gain the advantage by doing things before they need to be done—positioning yourself ahead of time. Enduring success is found when you travel in advance of the crowd. I believe one of the major benefits of reading the Bible is that it teaches us how to respond in advance to many of life's challenges and opportunities.

Dig a well before you're thirsty. Plant a seed before you're hungry. The trouble with the future for most people is it arrives before they are ready for it. Positioning yourself to receive causes you to be ready. The most important question is, *Are you ready?*

If You Don't Do It, You Don't Really Believe It

> People judge you by your actions, not your intentions. You may have a heart of gold, but so does a hard-boiled egg.
>
> Anonymous

A thousand words will not leave so lasting an impression as one deed. Action is the natural fruit of direction. Follow good intentions with appropriate actions. "If ye *know* these things, happy are ye if you *do* them" (John 13:17, italics added).

Prayer should never be an excuse for inaction. Sometimes, I believe the Lord speaks to us like He spoke to Moses when He said, "Quit praying and get the people moving! Forward, march!" (Exod. 14:15 TLB). If you don't take action, you don't *really* believe it. Most prayers are only going to be answered when you attach action to them. Decide in advance to act on the answers to your prayers.

Some people spend their whole life searching for what's right, but they can't seem to find any time to practice it. "Remember, too, that knowing what is right to do and then not doing it is sin" (James 4:17 TLB). Your life story is not written with a pen but with your actions. To *do* nothing is the way to *be* nothing.

> There is no idleness without a thousand troubles.
>
> Welsh proverb

The devil's number-one hope is not an active sinner but an inactive Christian. "The devil tempts some, but an idle man tempts the devil" (English proverb). Be sure to keep busy doing what's right so the devil may always find you occupied.

Action subdues fear. When we challenge our fears, we master them. When we wrestle with our problems, they lose their grip on us. When we dare to confront the things that scare us, we open the door to our liberty.

Momentum doesn't just happen. "The common conception is that motivation leads to action, but the reverse is true—action precedes motivation" (Robert McKain). "Don't wait to be motivated. Take the bull by the horns until you have him screaming for mercy" (Michael Cadena).

Laziness is a load. Nothing is more exhausting than searching for easy ways to make a living. Expectation is the idle man's income. Laziness keeps on and on, but soon enough it arrives at poverty. We are weakest when we try to get something for nothing. "Hard work brings prosperity; playing around brings poverty" (Prov. 28:19 TLB).

A person of words and not of deeds is like a flowerbed full of weeds. Don't let weeds grow around your dreams. To only dream of the person you would like to be is to waste the person you are. Some people dream of great accomplishments, while others stay awake and do them. Henry Ford commented, "You can't build a reputation on what you're going to do." "Shun idleness. It is a rust that attaches itself to the most brilliant of metals" (Voltaire).

Be a combination of a carrier pigeon and a woodpecker: don't just carry the message, but also knock on the door.

Get Up One More Time Than You've Fallen Down

Have you ever failed or made a mistake? Good, then this nugget is for you. The fact that you've failed is proof that you're not finished. Failures and mistakes can be a bridge, not a barricade, to success.

Psalm 37:23–24 says,

> The steps of a good man are ordered by the LORD: and he delighteth in his way. Though he fall, he shall not be utterly cast down: for the LORD *upholdeth him with his hand*. (italics added)

Failure may look like a fact, but it's only an opinion. Successful people believe that mistakes are just feedback. It's not how far you fall but how high you bounce that makes all the difference.

Theodore Roosevelt said,

> Far better it is to dare mighty things, to win glorious triumphs, even though checkered by failure, than to rank with those poor spirits who neither enjoy much nor suffer much because they live in the great twilight that knows not victory or defeat.

One of the riskiest things you can do in life is to take too many precautions and never have any failures or mistakes. Failure is the opportunity to start over more intelligently.

No one has ever achieved genuine success who did not, at one time or another, teeter on the edge of disaster. If you have tried to do something and failed, you are vastly better off than if you had tried to do nothing and succeeded. The person who never makes a mistake must get awfully tired of doing nothing. If you're not making mistakes, you're not risking enough.

Vernon Sanders observes,

> Experience is a hard teacher because she gives the test first, the lesson afterwards.

Experience is what you get when you are looking for something else.

Success consists of getting up just one time more than you fall down. So get up and go on.

"You don't drown by falling in the water, you drown by staying there," said author Ed Cole.

Proverbs 28:13 (TLB) reminds,

> A man who refuses to admit his mistakes can never be successful. But if he confesses and forsakes them, he gets another chance.

The death of your dream will not happen because of a failure; its death will come from indifference and apathy. The best way to go on after a failure is to learn the lesson and forget the details. If you don't, you'll become like the scalded dog that fears hot water and, afterward, fears cold as well.

Failure can become a weight, or it can give you wings. The only way to make a comeback is to go on. If the truth were known, 99 percent of success is built on former failure. A mistake usually proves somebody stopped talking long enough to do something. You're like a tea bag: not worth much until you've been through some hot water.

Remember the old poem:

> Success is failure turned inside out,
>   The silver tint of the clouds of doubt.
>   And you never can tell how close
>   you are;
>   It may be near when it seems so far.
> So stick to the fight when you're hardest hit;
>   It's when things seem worse
>   that you must not quit.
>
>   Unknown

There Is No Future in the Past

If you look back too much, you'll soon be heading that way. Mike Murdock said, "Stop looking at where you have been and start looking at where you can be." Your destiny and call in life is always forward, never backward. Katherine Mansfield advised,

> Make it a rule of life never to regret and never to look back. Regret is an appalling waste of energy. You can't build on it. It's only good for wallowing in.

Consider the words of the apostle Paul:

> Forgetting those things which are behind and reaching forward to those things which are

ahead, I press toward the goal for the prize
of the upward call of God in Christ Jesus.
Philippians 3:13–14 NKJV

You are more likely to make mistakes when you act only on past experiences. Rosy thoughts about the future can't exist when your mind is full of the blues about the past.

A farmer once said his mule was awfully backward about going forward—this is also true of many people today. Are you backward about going forward? Phillip Raskin said, "The man who wastes today lamenting yesterday will waste tomorrow lamenting today." Squash the "good old days" bug.

The past is always going to be the way it was. Stop trying to change it. Your future contains more happiness than any past you can remember. Believe that the best is yet to come.

Though no one can go back and make a brand new start, anyone can start from now and make a brand new ending.

Carl Bard

Consider Oscar Wilde:

> No man is rich enough to buy back his past.

Take note of what W. R. Ing said: "Events in the past may be roughly divided into those which probably never happened and those which do not matter." The more you look back, the less you will get ahead. Thomas Jefferson was right when he said, "I like the dreams of the future better than the history of the past." Many a has-been lives on the reputation of his reputation.

Hubert Humphrey mused,

> The good old days were never that good, believe me. The good new days are today, and better days are coming tomorrow. Our greatest songs are still unsung.

When you are depressed, you will find that it is because you are living in the past. What's a sure sign of stagnation in your life? When you dwell on the past at the expense of the future, you stop growing and start dying. Note Ecclesiastes 7:10 (NKJV):

Do not say,
"Why were the former days better
than these?"
For you do not inquire wisely
concerning this.

I agree with Laura Palmer's advice: "Don't waste today regretting yesterday instead of making a memory for tomorrow." David McNally reminded, "Your past cannot be changed, but you can change your tomorrow by your actions today." Never let yesterday use up too much of today. It's true what Satchel Paige said: "Don't look back. Something may be gaining on you."

"Living in the past is a dull and lonely business; looking back strains the neck muscles, causing you to bump into people not going your way" (Edna Ferber). The first rule for happiness is to *avoid lengthy thinking on the past*. Nothing is as far away as one hour ago. Charles Kettering added,

> You can't have a better tomorrow if you are thinking about yesterday all the time. Your past doesn't equal your future.

Procrastination Is the Fertilizer That Makes Difficulties Grow

Ask yourself: "If I don't take action now, what will it ultimately cost me?" When a procrastinator has finally made up his mind, the opportunity has usually passed by. Edwin Markum said,

> When duty comes a knocking at your gate,
>   Welcome him in; for if you bid him wait,
> He will depart only to come once more
>   And bring seven other duties to your door.

What you put off until tomorrow, you'll probably put off tomorrow too. Success comes to the man who does today what others were thinking of doing tomorrow. The lazier a man is, the more he is going to do the next day.

> All problems become smaller if you don't dodge them, but confront them. Touch a thistle timidly, and it pricks you; grasp it boldly, and its spines crumble.
>
> William Halsey

Wasting time wastes your life. Miguel de Cervantes pondered, "By the street of By and By, one arrives at the house of never." A lazy person doesn't go through life—he's pushed through it. "The wise man does at once what the fool does finally" (Balthasar Gracian).

"Someday" is not a day of the week. Doing nothing is the most tiresome job in the world. When you won't start, your difficulties won't stop. Tackle any difficulty now—the longer you wait the bigger it grows. Procrastinators never have small problems because they always wait until their problems grow up.

In the game of life nothing is less important than the score at halftime.

The tragedy of life is not that man loses, but that he almost wins.

Haywood Broun

Don't leave before the miracle happens! Robert Louis Stevenson commented that "saints are sinners who kept on going." The race is not always to the swift but to those who keep on running. Some people wait so long the future is gone before they get there.

The first step to overcoming procrastination is to eliminate all excuses for not taking action. The second step is not to be so busy! Everyone is always on the move. People are moving forward, backward, and sometimes nowhere at all, as though they were on a treadmill. The mistake most people make is in thinking that the main goal of life is to stay busy. This is a trap. What is important is not whether you are busy but whether you are progressing; the question is one of activity versus accomplishment.

A gentleman named John Henry Fabre conducted an experiment with processionary caterpillars, so named because they have a habit of blindly following each other no matter how they are lined up or where they are going. In his research, Fabre placed these tiny creatures in a circle. For twenty-four hours the caterpillars dutifully followed one another around and around and around. Then Fabre placed the caterpillars around a saucer full of pine needles (their favorite food). For six days the mindless creatures moved around and around the saucer, dying from starvation and exhaustion even though an abundance of choice food was located less than two inches away. The caterpillars were extremely active, but they were not accomplishing anything.

We should be known as those who accomplish great things for God—not as those who simply talk about it. Procrastinators are good at talking, not doing. Mark Twain said,

> Noise produces nothing. Often a hen who has merely laid an egg cackles as though she has laid an asteroid.

We must be like the apostles. These men are not known for their policies, procedures, theories, or excuses but for their acts. Many people say that they are waiting for God, but in most cases God is waiting for them. Together with the psalmist, we need to say, Lord, "my times are in your hands" (Ps. 31:15 NIV).

The cost of growth is always less than the cost of stagnation. As Edmund Burke warned,

> The only thing necessary for the triumph of evil is for good men to do nothing.

Occasionally you may see someone who doesn't do anything though appearing to be successful in life. Don't be deceived. Remember the old saying: "Even a broken clock is right twice a day."

Most people who sit around waiting for their ship to come in often find it is hardship. Those things that come to a man who waits seldom turn out to be the things he's waited for. The hardest work in the world is that which should have been done yesterday. Hard work is usually an accumulation of easy things that should have been done last week.

Sir Josiah Stamp said, "It is easy to dodge our responsibilities, but we cannot dodge the consequences of dodging our responsibilities." William James reflected, "Nothing is so fatiguing as the eternal hanging on of an uncompleted task." When people delay action until all factors are perfect, they do nothing. Jimmy Lyons mused, "Tomorrow is the only day in the year that appeals to a lazy man."

Procrastination is the grave in which opportunity is buried. Anybody who brags about what he's going to do tomorrow probably did the same thing yesterday. Few things are more dangerous to a person's character than having nothing to do and plenty of time in which to do it. Killing time is not murder, it's suicide. Two things rob people of their peace of mind: Work unfinished, and work not yet begun.

The Bible promises no loaves to the loafer.

A man with nothing to do does far more strenuous "labor" than any other form of

work. But my greatest pity is for the man
who dodges a job he knows he should do.
He is a shirker, and boy! What punishment
he takes . . . from himself.

E. R. Collcord

Carve out a future; don't just whittle away the
time.

Continually Frustrate Tradition with Your Creativity and Imagination

Stop and daydream once in a while. We all need to let our imaginations roam and give them a chance to breathe. It's never too late for you to start thinking more creatively.

Often it is merely a lack of imagination that keeps a person from his potential. Thinking of new ideas is like shaving: If you don't do it every day, you're a bum. Start and maintain a constant flow of new, exciting, and powerful ideas on which you act immediately.

Continually frustrate tradition with your creativity and imagination.

The opportunities of man are limited only by his imagination. But so few have imagination that there are ten thousand fiddlers to one composer.

Charles Kettering

Your dreams are a preview to your greatness. All men who have achieved great things have been dreamers. It may be that those who do most, dream most. A shallow thinker seldom makes a deep impression. We act, or fail to act, not because of *will*, as is so commonly believed, but because of *vision*. Only a person who sees the invisible can do the impossible.

Ideas are like rabbits. You get a couple and learn how to handle them, and pretty soon you have a dozen.

Anonymous

You'll get more out of every part of your life if you stay incurably curious. "The important thing is to not stop questioning. Never lose a holy curiosity" (Albert Einstein). Dexter Yager says, "Don't let anybody steal your dream."

"We've got to have a dream if we are going to make a dream come true" (Denis Waitley). Nothing happens unless there's a dream first. The more you can dream, the more you can do.

> Ideas are like the stars: we never reach them, but, like the mariners of the sea, we chart our course by them.
>
> Carl Schurz

God gave us a world unfinished so we might share in the joys and satisfaction of creation: "Creativity has been built into every one of us; it's part of our design. Each of us lives less of the life God intended for us when we choose not to live out the creative powers we possess" (Ted Engstrom).

> I'm a big fan of dreams. Unfortunately, dreams are the first casualty in life—people seem to give them up quicker than anything for a "reality."
>
> Kevin Costner

Realistic people with practical aims are rarely as realistic or practical in the long-run of life as the dreamers who pursue their dreams.

Hans Selye

What you need is an idea. Be brave enough to live creatively. "Since it doesn't cost a dime to dream, you'll never short-change yourself when you stretch your imagination" (Robert Schuller). A single idea—the sudden flash of any thought—may be worth a million dollars. Look at things not as they are but as they can be. Vision adds value to everything.

Only Hungry Minds
Can Grow

Have you ever noticed there are people you know who are literally at the same place today as they were five years ago? They still have the same dreams, the same problems, the same alibis, the same opportunities, and the same way of thinking. They are not moving forward in life.

It's as if they unplug their clocks at a certain point in time and stay at that fixed moment. However, God's will for us is to grow, to continue to learn and improve. The biggest room in our house is always the room for self-improvement.

A famous saying reads: "It's what you learn after you know it all that counts." I must admit that I am somewhat of a fanatic about this.

I hate to have idle time—time in which I am not learning anything. Those around me know that I must always have something to read or to write during any idle moment that might arise. In fact, I try to learn from everyone. From one I may learn what not to do, while from another I learn what to do. Learn from the mistakes of others. You can never live long enough to make all the mistakes yourself. You can learn more from a wise man when he is wrong than from a fool when he is right.

Goethe said, "Everybody wants to be: nobody wants to grow." I agree with Van Crouch:

> You will never change your actions until you
> change your mind.

An important way to keep growing is to never stop asking questions. The person who is afraid of asking is ashamed of learning. Life's most important answers can be found in asking the right questions.

We should learn as if we will live forever and live as if we will die tomorrow. It's true what

W. Fussellman said: "Today a reader. Tomorrow a leader." Harvey Ullman observed,

> Anyone who stops learning is old, whether this happens at 20 or 80. Anyone who keeps on learning not only remains young, but becomes consistently more valuable regardless of physical capacity.

Timothy is instructed: "Study to [show] thyself approved unto God" (2 Tim. 2:15). It's fun to keep learning. Learning brings approval to your life.

Learn from others. Learn to see in the challenges of others the ills you should avoid. Experience is a present possession that keeps us from repeating the past in the future. Life teaches us by giving us new problems before we solve the old ones. Do you believe that education is costly or difficult? Listen to Derek Bok:

> If you think education is expensive—try ignorance.

Do What Others Say Can't Be Done

Conservative talk-radio-show host Rush Limbaugh has a wonderful name for his outlandish tie collection—*No Boundaries*. What a great slogan this makes for living our lives. We should do what takes us out of our comfort zones. Be like David. Find a giant and slay it. Always pick an obstacle big enough that it matters when you overcome it.

Until you give yourself to some great cause, you haven't really begun to fully live. Henry Miller commented,

> The man who looks for security, even in the mind, is like a man who would chop off his limbs in order to have artificial ones which would never give him pain or trouble.

75

Nothing significant is ever accomplished by a fully realistic person.

Tradition offers no hope for the present and makes no preparation for the future. Day by day, year by year, broaden your horizon. Russell Davenport remarked,

> Progress in every age results only from the fact that there are some men and women who refuse to believe that what they know to be right cannot be done.

Know the rules and then break some. Take the lid off. Melvin Evans said,

> The men who build the future are those who know that greater things are yet to come, and that they themselves will help bring them about. The blazing sun of hope illumines their minds. They never stop to doubt. They haven't time.

Be involved in something bigger than you. God has never yet had any unqualified workers. "We are the wire, God is the current. Our only power is to let the current pass through it" (Carlo Carretto). Be a mind through which Christ thinks; a heart through which Christ loves; a voice through which Christ speaks; and a hand with which Christ helps.

If you really want to defend what you believe, live it. Dorothea Brand stated,

> All that is necessary to break the spell of inertia and frustration is this: act as if it were impossible to fail.

Do a right-about-face that turns you from failure to success. One of the greatest pleasures you can discover is doing what people say you cannot do.

Keep Your Temper—
Nobody Else Wants It

Don't fly into a rage unless you are prepared for a rough landing. Anger falls one letter short of danger. People constantly blowing fuses are generally left in the dark. If you lose your head, how can you expect to use it?

A Filipino saying advises: "Postpone today's anger until tomorrow." (Then apply this rule the next day and the next.) When you are upset, take a lesson from modern science: Always count down before blasting off. Seneca quipped, "The best cure for anger is delay." Proverbs 16:32 counsels,

> He who is slow to anger is better than
>   the mighty,

And he who rules his spirit than he who
takes a city. (NKJV)

Blowing your stack never fails to add to the air
pollution. How many great ideas have you had
while you were angry? How many "expensive
words" have you said when you were upset?
You'll never get to the top if you keep blowing
yours.

One of the worst fruits of anger is revenge.
No passion of the human heart promises so
much and pays so little as that of revenge. The
longest odds in the world are those against getting even with someone.

Instead of revenge, consider what the Bible
orders: "'Vengeance is Mine, I will repay,' says
the Lord. Therefore, 'If your enemy is hungry,
feed him; If he is thirsty, give him a drink; For
in so doing you will heap coals of fire on his
head'" (Rom. 12:19–20 NKJV). Francis Bacon
added,

> In taking revenge a man is but even with his
> enemies; but in passing it over, he is superior.

Marcus Antonius reflected, "Consider how much more you often suffer from your anger and grief than from those very things for which you are angry and grieved." David Hume said,

> He is happy whose circumstances suit his temper; but he is more excellent who can suit his temper to any circumstance.

Anger comes back to you, and it will surely hit you harder than anyone or anything at which you throw it.

Time spent in getting even is better used in trying to get ahead. Revenge is like biting a dog because the dog has bitten you. When trying to get even, you will always do odd and unhelpful things.

> Vengeance is a dish that should be eaten cold.
> Old English Proverb

Change, but Don't Stop

When you're through changing, you're through. Many people fail in life because they're unwilling to make changes. The fact is that correction and change always result in fruit.

All humankind is divided into three classes: Those that are unchangeable, those that are changeable, and those that cause change.

> Change is always hardest for the man who is in a rut. For he has scaled down his living to that which he can handle comfortably and welcomes no change or challenge that would lift him up.
>
> C. Neil Strait

If you find yourself in a hole, stop digging. When things go wrong—don't go with them.

Stubbornness and unwillingness to change is the energy of fools.

"He that will not apply new remedies must expect new evils" (Francis Bacon).

> I will instruct you (says the Lord) and guide you along the best pathway for your life; I will advise you and watch your progress.
>
> Psalm 32:8 TLB

God never closes one door without opening another one. We must be willing to change in order to walk through that new door. In prayer, we learn to change. Prayer is one of the most changing experiences we will ever know. You cannot pray and stay the same.

Playing it safe is probably the most unsafe thing in the world. You cannot stand still. You must go forward and be open to those adjustments that God has for you. The most unhappy people are those that fear change.

You can't make an omelet without breaking eggs. Accomplishment automatically results in change. One change makes way for the next, giving us the opportunity to grow. You must change to master change.

You've got to be open to change, because every time you think you're ready to graduate from the school of experience, somebody thinks up a new course. Decide to be willing to experience change. If you can figure where to stand firm and when to bend, you've got it made. Welcome change as a friend. We can become nervous because of incessant change, but we would be frightened if the change were stopped.

Blessed is the man who can adjust to a set of circumstances without surrendering his convictions. Open your arms to change, but don't let go of your values. People often meet with failure because of a lack of persistence in developing new ideas and lack of plans to take the place of those that failed. Your growth depends on your willingness to experience change.

Never Surrender
Your Dream to Noisy
Negatives

Nobody can ever make you feel average
without your permission. Ingratitude and
criticism are going to come; they are part of
the price you pay for leaping past mediocrity.

Jesus Himself, after healing ten lepers, was
thanked by only one of them (Luke 17:11–19).
Learn to expect ingratitude.

If you move with God, you will be critiqued.
The only way to avoid criticism is to do nothing
and be nothing. Those who do things inevitably
stir up criticism.

The Bible offers this great promise concerning

criticism: The truth always outlives a lie. This fact is backed by Proverbs 12:19:

> The lip of truth shall be established for ever:
> but a lying tongue is but for a moment.

Also, in Hebrews 13:6, we are told that "we may boldly say, 'The Lord is my helper, and I will not fear what man shall do unto me.'"

Never judge people by what is said about them by their enemies. Kenneth Tynan has provided the best description of a critic I have ever heard:

> A critic is a man who knows the way but can't drive the car.

We are not called to respond to criticism; we are called to respond to God. Often criticism will present the best platform from which to proclaim the truth.

Most of the time, people who are critical are either envious or uninformed. They usually say things that have no impact whatsoever upon truth. There's an anonymous saying that describes this situation perfectly:

> It is useless for the sheep to pass resolutions in favor of vegetarianism while the wolf remains of a different opinion.

If what you say and do is of God, it will not make any difference if every other person on the face of the earth criticizes you. Likewise, if what you are doing is not of God, nothing other people say will make it right.

Pay no attention to negative criticism. "Trust in the LORD, and do good" (Ps. 37:3), knowing that in the end what you do in the Lord will be rewarded.

All People Are Born Originals; Most Die as Copies

The call in your life is not to be a copy.

In this day of peer pressure, trends, and fads, we need to realize that each person has been custom-made by God the Creator. Each of us has a unique call. We should be ourselves.

Because I do a lot of work with churches, I come into contact with many different types of people. One time I talked over the phone with a pastor I had never met and who did not know me personally. We agreed that I would visit his church as a consultant, and as we were closing our conversation and were setting a time to meet at the local airport, he asked me,

"How will I know you when you get off the plane?"

"Oh, don't worry, Pastor—I'll know you," I responded jokingly. "All pastors look alike."

The point of this story is that you must be the person God has made *you* to be.

You and I can always find someone richer than we are, poorer than we are, or more or less able than we are. But how other people are, what they have, and what happens in their lives have no effect upon our call. In Galatians 6:4 (TLB) we are admonished,

> Let everyone be sure that he is doing his very best, for then he will have the personal satisfaction of work well done and won't need to compare himself with someone else.

God made you a certain way. You are unique, one of a kind. To copy others is to cheat yourself out of the fullness of what God has called you to be and to do. Imitation is limitation.

Stand out; don't blend in. The majority, many times, is a group of highly motivated snails. If a thousand people say something foolish, it is still foolish. Truth is never dependent upon consensus of belief.

Don't be persuaded or dissuaded by group opinion. It does not make any difference what anyone else believes; you must believe. Never take direction for your personal life from a crowd. Never choose to quit just because somebody disagrees with you. In fact, the two worst things you can say to yourself when you get an idea is "That's never been done before!" and "That's been done before!"

First Peter 2:9 says of us Christians,

> You are a chosen generation, a royal priesthood, a holy nation, His own special people, that you may proclaim the praises of Him who called you out of darkness into His marvelous light. (NKJV)

Romans 12:2 exhorts us,

> Do not conform to the pattern of this world, but be transformed by the renewing of your mind. Then you will be able to test and

approve what God's will is—his good, pleasing and perfect will. (NIV)

Christians live in this world, but we are aliens. We should talk differently, act differently, and perform differently. We should stand out.

There should be something different about you. If you do not stand out in a group, if your life is not unique or different, you should re-evaluate yourself.

Choose to accept and become the person God has made you to be. Tap into the originality and creative genius of God in your life. If you're not you, then who are you going to be?

Part Two

LOOKING

OUTWARD

From This Page
You Can Go Anywhere
You Want To

Do you know what this page is noted for? This page is the springboard to your future. It's a starting point for any place in the world. You can start here and go anywhere you want to.

God has placed within each of us the potential and opportunity for success. It takes just as much effort and energy for a bad life as it does for a good life. Still, millions lead aimless lives in a prison of their own making—simply because they haven't decided what to do with their lives. It always costs more not to do God's will than to do it. In fact, "A lot of people confuse bad decision-making with destiny" (Kin Hubbard).

When you accept God's original construction for your life, you shine like a star in the night. When you choose to be a copy, you're like the darkness of the night. You can predict a person's future by their awareness of their purpose. Life's heaviest burden is to have nothing to carry. A person's significance is determined by the cause for which they live and the price they are willing to pay.

How would you like to spend two years making phone calls to people who aren't home? Sound absurd? According to one time-management study, that's how much time the average person spends over a lifetime trying to return calls to people who never seem to be in. Not only that, we spend six months waiting for the traffic light to turn green and another eight months reading junk mail. These unusual statistics should cause us to "number our days" as the Bible tells us (Ps. 90:12).

Don't waste one of your most precious commodities . . . time. Each minute is an irretrievable gift—an unrestorable slice of history. Realize that now is the best time to do what you're supposed to do!

What you set your heart on will determine how you spend your life. So be moved by conviction, not ego.

> Learning to praise God after the answer is obedience. Learning to praise God before the answer is faith. Obedience is good, but faith moves God.
>
> Bob Harrison

Faith builds a bridge from this world to the next. Before you can go high you must first go deep.

No wind blows in favor of a ship without a destination. A person without a purpose is like a ship without a rudder. What you set your heart on will determine how you'll spend your life. A person going nowhere can be sure of reaching that destination. Be called and sent—not up and went. God plants no yearning in your heart He doesn't plan to satisfy. Sadly, we distrust our hearts too much and our heads not enough.

Jesus, a man of purpose, once said, "To this end was I born, and for this cause came I into the world, that I should bear witness unto the truth" (John 18:37). Better to die for something than to live for nothing.

You're Created for Connection

God didn't write solo parts for us. He has divine connections for you—right friends and associations. These good relationships always bring out the original in you. You know the kind of people I'm talking about; after you've been with them you find yourself less critical, full of faith, and having a vision for the future. So respect those God has assigned to help you. The worth of any relationship can by measured by its contribution to your vision, plan, or purpose. Someone is always observing you who is capable of greatly blessing you.

It's very important whom we closely associate with. Have you ever known a backslider who didn't first hang around with the wrong kind of people? The devil doesn't use strangers to deter or stop you. These wrong associations bring out the worst in you, not the best. After you're around them you'll find yourself full of doubt, fear, confusion, and criticism. The devil's favorite entry into your life is usually through those you are closest to.

As you grow in God, your associations will change. Some of your friends won't want you to grow. They'll want you to stay where they are. Friends who don't help you climb will want you to crawl. Your friends will either stretch your vision or choke your dream.

Never let anyone talk you out of pursuing a God-given idea. "Don't let someone else create your world for you, for when they do they always make it too small" (Ed Cole). Who's creating your world?

Never receive counsel from unproductive people. Never discuss your problems with someone incapable of contributing to the solution. Those who never succeed themselves are always first to tell you how.

Not everyone has a right to speak into your life.

Once upon a time, a beautiful, independent, self-assured princess happened upon a frog in a pond. The frog said to the princess, "I was once a handsome prince until an evil witch put a spell on me. One kiss from you and I will turn back into a prince. Then we can marry and move into the castle with my mom. You can prepare my meals, clean my clothes, bear my children, and forever feel happy doing so."

Later that night, while the princess dined on frog legs, she kept laughing and saying, "I don't think so!" Remember, not everyone has a right to speak into your life . . . so stop letting them.

You are certain to get the worst of the bargain when you exchange ideas with the wrong person. I like to put it this way: don't follow anyone who's not going anywhere. We are to follow no person farther than he or she follows Jesus.

Mike Murdock says, "When God gets ready to bless you, He brings a person into your life." God cares for people through people.

With some people you spend an evening; with others you invest it. Be careful where you stop to inquire for directions along the road of your life. Wise is the person who fortifies life with the right friendships.

Failure Is Waiting
on the Path of
Least Persistence

Never give up on what you know you really should do. A person with big dreams is more powerful than one with all the facts. Remember, overnight success takes about ten years. The "person of the hour" spent many days and nights getting there. Like a friend of mine once said, "My overnight success was the longest night of my life." Winners simply do what losers don't want to do longer.

Earl Nightingale tells of a young man who once asked a great and famous older man, "How can I make a name for myself in the world and become successful?" The great and famous man replied, "You have only to decide upon what it is you want and then stay with it, never deviating from your course no matter how long it takes, or how rough the road, until you have accomplished it." Success seems to be largely a matter of holding on after others have let go.

In the confrontation between the stream and the rock, the stream always wins—not through strength but perseverance. Christopher Morley said, "Big shots are only little shots that keep shooting." Endurance, patience, and commitment mean enjoying the distance between God's promises and His provision for your life. "The desire accomplished is sweet to the soul" (Prov. 13:19). Persistence may be bitter, but its fruit is sweet.

Judas, who betrayed Jesus, was an example of someone who began the good fight of faith but lacked persistence. Many of the world's great failures did not realize how close they were to success when they gave up. Stopping at third base adds no more to the score than striking out. We rate success by what people finish, not by what they start.

The secret of success is to start from scratch and keep on scratching. In his book *The Sower's Seeds*, Joel Weldon talks about the Moso, a bamboo plant that grows in China and the Far East. "After the Moso is planted, no visible growth occurs for up to five years—even under ideal conditions! Then, as if by magic, it suddenly begins growing at the rate of nearly two and one half feet per day, reaching a full height of ninety feet within six weeks! But it's not magic. The Moso's rapid growth is due to the miles of roots it develops during those first five years . . . five years of getting ready." Did this plant really grow ninety feet in six weeks or did it grow ninety feet in five years? Of course, the answer is five years. If at any time in those five years the seed had been without water, fertilizer, and nurture, the Moso plant would have died. People do not fail, they just quit too early.

God won't give up on you! Don't you give up on God. "For I am persuaded, that neither death, nor life, nor angels, nor principalities, nor powers, nor things present, nor things to come, nor height, nor depth, nor any other creature, shall be able to separate us from the love of God, which is in Christ Jesus our Lord" (Rom. 8:38–39).

Your persistence is proof you've not yet been defeated. Therefore, "Commit to the LORD whatever you do, and he will establish your plans" (Prov. 16:3 NIV). Life holds no greater wealth than steadfast commitment. It cannot be robbed from you. Only you can lose it by your lack of will.

> You have no right to anything you have not pursued. For the proof of desire is in the pursuit.
>
> Mike Murdock

The destiny of the diligent is to stand in the company of leaders. "Seest thou a man diligent in his business? He shall stand before kings" (Prov. 22:29). When faithfulness is most difficult, it's most necessary. Trying times are no time to quit trying. Enduring is a military term meaning to hold up courageously under fire. When you feel like quitting, bring more of God into that area of your life.

The Sky's Not the Limit

No one can put a limit on you without your permission. It was because of their attitudes—not the giants—that the Israelites didn't enter the promised land.

Eli Whitney was laughed at when he showed his cotton gin. Edison had to install his electric light free of charge in an office building before anyone would even look at it. The first sewing machine was smashed to pieces by a Boston mob. People scoffed at the idea of railroads. People thought traveling thirty miles an hour would stop the circulation of the blood. Morse had to plead before ten Congresses before they would even look at his telegraph. Yet for all these men the sky was not the limit.

> Beware of those who stand aloof
> And greet each venture with reproof.

The world would stop if things were run
By men who say "It can't be done."

Anonymous

Jesus tells us, "Seek, and ye shall find" (Matt. 7:7). We attain only in proportion to what we attempt. More people are persuaded to believe in nothing than to believe in too much. As Jesus told the blind men, "According to your faith be it unto you" (Matt. 9:29). You are never as far from the answer as it first appears. It's never safe or accurate to look into the future without faith.

So how can you find? You must seek. Tell me what you believe about Jesus and I can tell some important facts about your future. What picture of Jesus do you have? Was He merely a good man with good ideas? Or is He the Son of the living God, our advocate before the Father, the King of Kings and Lord of Lords?

Be more concerned about what the still small voice whispers than about what other people shout. A lot of people no longer hope for the best, they just hope to avoid the worst. Many of us have heard opportunity knocking at our door, but by the time we unhooked the chain, pushed back the bolt, turned two locks, and shut off the burglar alarm—it was gone! Too many people spend their lives looking around, looking down, or looking behind. God says, *Look up*. The sky's not the limit.

What Good Is Aim If You Don't Know When to Pull the Trigger?

God is a God of timing *and* direction. He wants us to know what to do and when to do it. In Psalm 32:8 He promises, "I will instruct thee and teach thee in the way which thou shalt go: I will guide thee with mine eye." Don't live your life ahead or outside of His will.

Patience will do wonders, but it wasn't much help to the man who planted an orange grove in Alaska. There's never a right time to do the wrong thing. If you take too long in deciding what to do with your life, you'll find you've lived it. Time was invented by almighty God in order to give dreams a chance. "Hell is truth

seen too late—duty neglected in its season"
(Tryon Edwards). Ideas won't keep . . . something must be done about them.

> There is one thing stronger than all the armies
> in the world, and that is an idea whose time
> has come.
>
> Victor Hugo

One cool judgment is worth a thousand hasty
judgments. When Billy Graham got off an airplane one day, there was a limousine waiting for
him. Even though he was over ninety years old,
he walked up to the limousine driver and said,
"You know what, I've never driven a limousine
before. I want to drive the limousine."

The driver said, "Okay, I'll let you drive it." So
Billy Graham got into the limousine and started
driving. He wasn't used to driving a limousine,
and soon was going 70 miles an hour in a 55-mile-
an-hour zone. A rookie policeman pulled him
over, walked up to the car, looked in, and saw
Dr. Billy Graham. The policeman was a little
nervous as he said, "May I see your license, sir?"

He looked at the license, and sure enough—it was Dr. Billy Graham.

The rookie walked back to his squad car, called headquarters, and said, "Look, I have just stopped a very, very important individual."

"How important is he?" came the reply from headquarters.

"Well, he's very important."

"Is he more important than the governor?"

"He's more important than the governor."

"Is it the president of the United States?"

"He's more important than the president of the United States."

"Well, who is it?"

"Well, I think it's the Lord because Billy Graham is his chauffeur."

Jumping to a wrong decision seldom leads to a happy landing. Too many people leave the right opportunity to look for other opportunities. Seize today's opportunities today and tomorrow's opportunities tomorrow.

Always apply light, not heat, to your dreams. God teaches us that His Word is a lamp unto our feet and a light unto our path (see Ps. 119:105). The lamp illuminates things we are dealing with close at hand. The light on our path enlightens our future direction.

Don't hurry when success depends on accuracy. Those who make the worst use of their time are the first to complain of its shortness. The fastest running back is useless unless heading toward the right goal line.

Timing is the vital ingredient for success. "For the vision is yet for an appointed time" (Hab. 2:3). There is an appointed time for your vision. Have 20/20 vision. Don't be too farsighted or too nearsighted. As I've studied godly leaders, I've found at key times they have said, "God lead me to do . . ." Obedience to God's will is the GPS on the road of His plan for you.

Following His perfect will releases the originality within you and helps you identify priorities. If Jesus is the Way, why waste time traveling some other way?

When Others
Throw Bricks
at You, Turn Them
into Stepping-Stones

All great ideas create conflict, battle, and wars. In other words, your destiny creates challenges and criticism.

Every great, big, and unique idea has three stages of responses:

> "It's impossible—don't waste the time and the money."
>
> "It's possible but has a limited value."
>
> "I said it was a good idea all along."

Our response to critics should be what Paul says: "We are perplexed, but not in despair;

persecuted, but not forsaken; cast down, but not destroyed" (2 Cor. 4:8–9). Love your enemies, but if you really want to make them mad, ignore them completely.

Criticism of Christians is the language of the devil. The Bible describes the devil as the accuser of the brethren. Therefore, we should consider Jesus's words: "He that is without sin among you, let him first cast a stone" (John 8:7). Bees can't make honey and sting at the same time. Attention men: before you criticize another, look closely at your sister's brother!

We should heed the still small voice, not the deafening blasts of doom. If your head sticks up above the crowd, expect more criticism than bouquets. Satan always attacks those who can hurt him the most. God works from the inside out; the devil tries to work from the outside in.

Whoever criticizes *to* you will criticize *about* you. A person who belittles you is only trying to cut you down to his or her size. A critic is one who finds fault without a search warrant. A statue has never been set up to a critic.

A bus carrying only ugly people crashes into an oncoming truck, and everyone inside dies. As they stand at the pearly gates waiting to enter paradise and meet their maker, God decides to grant each person one wish because of the grief they have experienced.

They're all lined up, and God asks the first person to make a wish. "I want to be gorgeous," and so God snaps His fingers and it is done.

The second one in line hears this and says, "I want to be gorgeous too." Another snap of God's fingers and the wish is granted.

This goes on for a while, with each one asking to be gorgeous. But when God is halfway down the line, the last guy in the line starts laughing. When there are only ten people left, this guy is rolling on the floor, laughing his head off.

Finally, God reaches this last guy and asks him what his wish will be. The guy eventually calms down and says, "Make 'em all ugly again."

You can always tell a failure by the way he or she criticizes success. Failures never offer a better solution to a problem. Those who can—do. Those who can't—criticize. Those who complain about the way the ball bounces are often the ones who dropped it. If it weren't for the doers, the critics would soon be out of business. Envy provides the mud that failures throw at success. Those who are throwing mud are simultaneously losing mud. Small minds are the first to criticize large ideas.

If people talk negatively about you, live so no one will believe them. Fear of criticism is the kiss of death in the courtship of achievement. If you're afraid of criticism, you'll die doing nothing. A successful person is someone who can lay a firm foundation with the bricks others throw at them.

There's No Such Thing as a Self-Made Person

No one can make it alone. Remember, if you try to go it alone, the fence that shuts others out also shuts you in. "God sends no one away except those who are full of themselves" (D. L. Moody). The person who only works by themselves and for themselves is likely to be corrupted by the company they keep.

There is no such thing as a "self-made" man or woman. We are made up of thousands of others.

> Everyone who has ever done a kind deed for us or spoken one word of encouragement to us has entered into the make-up of our character and of our thoughts, as well as our success.
> George Matthew Adams

Have a grateful heart and be quick to acknowledge those who help you. Make yourself indispensable to somebody. It's easy to blame others for your failures, but do you credit others with your successes?

"Tunnel vision tells you nobody is working as hard as you are. Tunnel vision is an enemy of teamwork. It's a door through which division and strife enter" (Tim Redmond). Few burdens are heavy when everybody lifts. Freckles would make a nice coat of tan if they would get together.

Everyone needs someone. An elderly couple walked into a fast-food restaurant. The little old man walked up to the counter, ordered the food, paid, and took the tray back to the table where the little old lady sat. On the tray was a hamburger, a small bag of fries, and a drink.

Carefully, the old man cut the hamburger in two and divided the fries into two neat piles. He sipped the drink and passed it to the little old lady, who took a sip and passed it back.

A young man at a nearby table had watched the old couple and felt sorry for them. He offered to buy them another meal, but the old man politely declined, saying that they were used to sharing everything. The old man began to eat his food, but his wife sat still, not eating.

The young man continued to watch the couple. He still felt he should be offering to help. As the little old man finished eating, the old lady had still not started on her food. "Ma'am, why aren't you eating?" asked the young man sympathetically.

The old lady looked up and said politely, "I'm waiting for the teeth." We all need help from someone . . .

If you believe in nothing but yourself, you live in a very small world—one in which few will want to enter. The one who sings one's own praises may have the right tune but the wrong words. Conceited people never get anywhere because they think they're already there.

Every great person is always being helped by somebody. The higher you go in life, the more dependent you will become on other people. Woodrow Wilson was quoted as saying, "I not only use all the brains I have, but all that I can borrow." Behind a capable person there are always other capable people.

Work together with others. Remember the banana—every time it leaves the bunch, it gets peeled and eaten. You'll never experience lasting success without relationships. No one person alone can match the cooperative effort of the right team.

Don't Measure Yourself
with Another's Coat

A heart surgeon took his car to the local garage for a regular service. While he waited, he usually exchanged a little friendly banter with the owner, a skilled but not especially wealthy mechanic.

"So tell me," said the mechanic, "I've been wondering about what we both do for a living, and how much more you get paid than me."

"Yes?" said the surgeon.

"Well, look at this," said the mechanic, as he worked on a big, complicated engine. "I check how it's running, open it up, fix the valves, and put it all back together so it works good as new. We basically do the same job, don't we? And yet you are paid ten times what I am—how do you explain that?"

The surgeon thought for a moment, then smiling gently he replied, "Try it with the engine running."

"Every man must do two things alone. He must do his own believing and his own dying" (Martin Luther). When you compare yourself with others, you'll become either bitter or vain. There are always greater and lesser persons than you. Making comparisons is a sure path to frustration, but *comparison is never proof*. "You can't clear your own fields while counting the rocks on your neighbor's farm" (Joan Welch). "The grass may be greener on the other side of the fence, but there's probably more of it to mow" (Lois Cory). Hills look small and green a long way off.

You waste your energy, time, and effort when you compare yourself to others. What happens in another person's life has no impact and no effect on what happens in yours.

I was dismayed when I heard from a friend I hadn't seen for three or four years. He told me he felt bad in *his* life because of some of the success that had happened in *mine*. I couldn't help being perplexed at his comments, and I responded to him by saying, "Do you mean you would have felt a lot better if I'd done horribly the last three or four years?" Well, of course he said no. It just points out the fact that what's happening in another person's life is not a basis for how good or how bad you're doing in your own. Success in someone else's life doesn't hurt the chances for success in yours.

Life is more fun when you don't keep score for others. When you compare your place and plan with others, they're never accurate. *Nothing is as it appears!*

Success is simply a matter of doing what you do best and not worrying about what the other person is going to do. You carry success or failure within yourself; it doesn't depend on outside conditions.

Ask yourself the question Earl Nightingale once posed: "Are you motivated by what you really want out of life, or are you mass-motivated?" Make sure you decide what you really want, not what someone else wants for you. Do you say, "I'm good, but not as good as I ought to be"? Or do you say, "I'm not as bad as a lot of other people"? The longer you dwell on another's weakness, the more you affect your own mind with unhappiness. You must create your own system, your own plan, or you'll be enslaved by another person's. Don't reason and compare. Your purpose is to create, not re-create.

"We only become what we are by the radical and deep-seated refusal of that which others have made of us" (Jean-Paul Sartre). Every person who trims himself to suit everybody else will soon find himself whittled away. So don't measure your situation against that of others. Measure your situation against God's Word and His will for your life.

If a thousand people say a foolish thing, it is still a foolish thing. Direction from God is never a matter of consensus or public opinion. A wise man makes his own decision; an ignorant man follows public opinion. Don't think you're necessarily on the right road just because it's a well-beaten path. The greatest risk in life is to wait for and depend on others for your security. Don't measure yourself with another man's coat. Don't judge yourself through someone else's eyes.

Invest in Others

One of the most exciting decisions you can make is to be on the lookout for opportunities to invest in others. For me, this has been one of the most powerful principles of momentum I've implemented in my life.

I remember driving with my family from St. Louis to Tulsa, Oklahoma. I was listening to a Zig Ziglar audio book. He said, "You'll always have everything you want in life if you'll help enough others get what they want." When I heard this statement, something literally went off inside of me and I said out loud, "I'm going to do it. I'm going to aggressively help as many people as I can to get what they want out of life." That decision to look for ways to help others, to invest in them, changed my life and continues today.

One of the marks of true greatness is to develop greatness in others. "There are three keys to more abundant living: caring about others, daring for others, and sharing with others" (William Ward). I've found that really great leaders have a unique perspective. They understand that greatness is not deposited in them to stay but rather to flow through them into others. "We make a living by what we get, but we make a life by what we give" (Norman MacEwan). Assign yourself the purpose of making others happy and thereby give yourself a gift.

People have a way of becoming what you encourage them to be. Be sincerely interested in helping others. Ralph Waldo Emerson observed, "Trust men and they will be true to you; treat them greatly and they will show themselves great." Spend your life lifting people up, not putting people down. "Treat people as if they were what they ought to be and you help them to become what they are capable of being" (Goethe).

Whatever we praise, we increase. There's no investment you can make that will pay you so well as the effort to scatter sunshine and good cheer into others throughout your life journey.

The person who renders loyal service in a humble capacity will be chosen for higher responsibilities, just as the biblical servant who multiplied the one pound given by his master was made ruler over ten cities.

B. C. Forbes

There are two types of people in the world: those who come into a room and say, "Here I am!" and those who come in and say, "Ah, there you are!" How do you know a good person? A good person makes others good. Find happiness by helping others find it.

The story goes that over two hundred years ago, a man dressed in civilian clothes rode past a field where a small group of exhausted, battle-weary soldiers were digging an obviously important defensive position. Their section leader, himself making no effort to help, was shouting orders, threatening punishment if the work was not completed within the hour.

"Why are you not helping?" asked the stranger on horseback.

"I am in charge. The men do as I tell them," said the section leader. Then he added, "Help them yourself if you feel strongly about it."

To the section leader's surprise, the stranger dismounted and helped the men until the job was finished.

Before leaving, the stranger congratulated the men for their work and approached the puzzled section leader.

"You should notify top command next time your rank prevents you from supporting your men—and I will provide a more permanent solution," said the stranger.

Up close, the section leader now recognized General George Washington—and also the lesson he'd just been taught.

"What you make happen for others, God will make happen for you" (Mike Murdock). "Knowing that whatsoever good thing any man

129

doeth, the same shall he receive of the Lord"
(Eph. 6:8). A good deed bears interest. You
cannot hold a light to another's path without
brightening your own. Develop greatness in
others.

> There is no more noble occupation in the
> world than to assist another human being—
> to help someone succeed.
>
> Allan McGinnis

> The true meaning of life is to plant trees
> under whose shade you do not expect to sit.
>
> Nelson Henderson

The greatest use of your life is to spend it for
something and on someone who will outlast it.
"If you cannot win, make the one ahead of you
break the record" (Jan McKeithen).

Invest in others. It pays great dividends.

You Don't Learn Anything While You're Talking

One of the best ways to persuade others is by listening to them. You'll find a gossip talks to you about others, a bore talks to you about himself, and a brilliant conversationalist talks to you about yourself and listens to what you say. You don't learn anything while you're talking. The truth is, the more you say the less people remember. When it comes to listening, it's always more blessed to receive than to give.

"Keep your mouth closed and you'll stay out of trouble" (Prov. 21:23 TLB). A person is known by the silence he or she keeps. Don't miss many valuable opportunities to hold your tongue and listen to what the other person is saying. When you have nothing to say, say nothing. Silence is a friend who will never betray you.

The greatest skill you can develop is the skill of listening to others. Say as little as possible to get the point across.

The obituary department of a local newspaper received a phone call one day. The caller asked, "How much do funeral notices cost?"

"Five dollars per word, ma'am," came the operator's response.

"Good. Do you have a paper and pencil handy?"

"Yes, ma'am."

"Okay, write this: 'Fred dead.'"

"I'm sorry, ma'am; I forgot to tell you there's a five-word minimum."

"Humph," came the reply. "You certainly did forget to tell me that."

A moment of silence.

"Got your pencil and paper?"

"Yes, ma'am."

"Okay, print this: 'Fred dead, Cadillac for sale.'"

> The man of few words and settled mind is wise; therefore, even a fool is thought to be wise when he is silent. It pays him to keep his mouth shut.
>
> Proverbs 17:27–28 TLB

Talk is cheap because supply exceeds demand. "As you go through life, you're going to have many opportunities to keep your mouth shut. Take advantage of all of them" (*West Virginia Gazette*). There must have been some reason God made human ears to stay open and human mouths to shut. As one grows older and wiser, one talks less and says more.

Learn to listen. Sometimes opportunity disguises itself this way and knocks very softly. You will find that God speaks for those who hold their peace. Silence can be golden.

Too much talk always includes error. There is only one rule for being a good talker: be a good listener. Your ears will never get you into trouble. One of the most powerful principles you can implement in your life is the principle of listening to others. "Don't talk so much. You keep putting your foot in your mouth. Be sensible and turn off the flow!" (Prov. 10:19 TLB).

Don't Let Things
Stick to You

As I've had the privilege of meeting hundreds of people over the past several years, one thing that always stood out to me is how many people have things attached to them. People allow a critical statement made by a third grade teacher, a failure or mistake they made ten or fifteen years ago, or the comments a noisy, negative neighbor made last week to hold them back from their destiny.

Only a foolish person adheres to all she hears. *Not everyone has a right to speak into your life.* This is one of the most powerful principles you can apply to acquire momentum.

I really believe one of the major benefits of asking forgiveness from God is that things no longer "stick" to us. He says that if we confess our sins, He is faithful and just to forgive us of our sins. That would be great enough, but incredibly God doesn't stop there. He also promises to cleanse us from all unrighteousness (see 1 John 1:9). When He cleanses us, we have a right standing before the Father. Why? He doesn't want things to stick to us. Because of our right standing before the Father, we're now free of the failures and mistakes, the wrong words and attitudes of the past, and we are released to accomplish things for the future.

I've found that successful people have a way of not letting things stick to them.

One Sunday morning before the services began, people were sitting in their pews and talking about their lives, their families, and so forth. Suddenly the devil appeared at the front of the church. Everyone started screaming and running for the exit, trampling one another in a frantic effort to get away from him.

Soon everyone was evacuated from the church except for one elderly gentleman who sat calmly in his pew, not moving . . . seemingly oblivious to the fact that God's ultimate enemy was in his presence.

Now this confused Satan a bit, so he walked up to the man and said, "Don't you know who I am?"

The man replied, "Yep, sure do."

Satan asked, "Aren't you afraid of me?"

"Nope, sure ain't," said the man.

Satan was a little perturbed at this and queried, "Why aren't you afraid of me?"

The man calmly replied, "Been married to your sister for over forty-eight years."

Like this elderly man, don't let stuff stick to you.

Don't worry if you don't get what you think you should. What seems so necessary today might not even be desirable tomorrow. "In times like these, it helps to recall that there have always been times like these" (Paul Harvey). If we could forget our troubles as easily as we forget our blessings, how different things would be.

One way to be free of things that want to stick to you is to take your mind off the things that seem to be against you. Thinking about these negative factors builds into them a power they don't truly possess. Talking about your grievances merely adds to those grievances.

Attach yourself to God's forgiveness, to His plan, and to His Word. Then watch yourself become loosed from former "sticky" situations.

Be the First to Forgive

Living a life of unforgiveness is like driving your car with your parking brake on. It causes you to slow down and lose your momentum. And you end up being worn out!

One of the most expensive luxuries you can possess is to be unforgiving toward someone. A deep-seated grudge in your life eats away at your peace of mind like a deadly cancer, destroying a vital organ of life. In fact, there are few things as pathetic and terrible to behold as a person who has harbored a grudge for many years.

The heaviest load you can possibly carry is a pack of grudges. So if you want to travel far and fast, then travel light. Unpack all of your envy, jealousy, unforgiveness, revenge, and fear.

Never reject forgiveness or the opportunity to forgive. The weak can never forgive because forgiveness is a characteristic of the strong. When you live a life of unforgiveness, revenge naturally follows. But revenge is the deceiver. It looks sweet, but it's most often bitter. It always costs more to revenge a wrong than to bear it. You can't win by trying to even the score.

Be the first to forgive. Forgiveness can be your deepest need and highest achievement. Many times it's the first step of an answer to prayer or release of a miracle. Without forgiveness, life is governed by an endless cycle of resentment and retaliation. What a dreadful waste of effort. "He who has not forgiven an enemy has never yet tasted one of the most sublime enjoyments of life," declares Johann Lavater.

Forgiving those who have wronged you is a key to your personal peace. What the world needs is peace that passes all *mis*understanding. Forgiveness also releases you for action and freedom.

"Never cut what can be untied" (Joseph Jobert). Don't burn bridges. You'll be surprised how many times you have to cross over that same river. Unforgiveness is empty, but forgiveness makes a future possible. You'll "get out of the right side of the bed" and "start your day on the right foot" if you ask yourself every day, "Whom do I need to forgive?"

There Are Good Ships and Bad Ships, but the Best Ships Are Friendships

Who you choose to be your closest friends or associates is one of the most important decisions you make during the course of your life. "You are the same today that you are going to be five years from now except for two things: the people with whom you associate and the books you read" (Charlie "Tremendous" Jones). The Bible says if you associate with wise men you'll become wise, but a companion of fools will be destroyed (see Prov. 13:20). You do become like those with whom you closely associate.

"Friends in your life are like pillars on your porch. Sometimes they hold you up, sometimes they lean on you, and sometimes it's just enough to know they're standing by" (Anonymous). "Iron sharpeneth iron; so a man sharpeneth the countenance of his friend" (Prov. 27:17). A real friend is a person who, when you've made a fool of yourself, let's you forget it. Good friendship always multiplies your joy and divides your grief.

I've found that the best friends are those who bring out the best in you, and a real good friend is someone who knows all about you and likes you anyway. A true friend is someone who is there for you when they'd rather be somewhere else. "A friend loveth at all times, and a brother is born for adversity" (Prov. 17:17). I believe we should keep our friendships in constant repair. In addition to loving our enemies, we should remember to treat our friends well too.

The wrong kind of friends, unlike the good kind of friends, brings out the worst, not the best, in you. You know the kind I'm talking about. They're the people who absorb sunshine and radiate gloom. The fact is not everyone will want you to succeed, no matter how hard you try.

An elderly man lay dying in his bed. In death's agony, he suddenly smelled the aroma of his favorite chocolate chip cookies wafting up the stairs. He gathered his remaining strength and lifted himself from his bed. Leaning against the wall, he slowly made his way out of his bedroom, and with even greater effort forced himself down the stairs, gripping the railing with both hands. With labored breath, he leaned against the doorframe while gazing into the kitchen.

Were it not for death's agony, he would have thought himself already in heaven. There, spread out on newspapers on the kitchen table, were literally hundreds of his favorite chocolate chip cookies. Was it heaven? Or was it one final act of heroic love from his devoted wife, seeing to it that he left this world a happy man?

Mustering one great final effort, he threw himself toward the table, landing on his knees in a rumpled posture. His parched lips parted;

the wondrous taste of the cookie was already in his mouth, seemingly bringing him back to life. His aged, withered, shaking hand made its way to a cookie at the edge of the table, when his wife suddenly smacked it with a spatula. "Stay out of those," she said. "They're for the funeral."

There are people who will always come up with reasons why you can't do what you know you're supposed to do. *Ignore them!* The Bible says in Proverbs 25:19, "Putting confidence in an unreliable man is like chewing with a sore tooth, or trying to run on a broken foot" (TLB).

A day away from the wrong associations is like a month in the country. "Keep away from people who try to belittle your ambitions. Small people always do that, but the really great make you feel that you, too, can become great" (Mark Twain). Never have a companion who casts you in the shade.

True friends don't sympathize with your weakness—they help summon your strength. "Treat your friends as you do your best pictures, and place them in their best light" (Jennie Churchill). Friends communicate at the heart level. There are good ships and there are bad ships, but the best ships are friendships.

A good friend never gets in your way . . . unless you're on your way down. A good friend is one who walks in when others walk out. The right kind of friends are those with whom you can dare to be yourself and with whom you can dream out loud. For me, my best friends are those who understand my past, believe in my future, and accept me today just the way I am.

Pick a Problem
Bigger Than You

People nearly always pick a problem their own size and ignore or leave to others the bigger or smaller ones. Pick a problem bigger than you. "Success—real success—in any endeavor demands more from an individual than most people are willing to offer—not more than they are capable of offering" (James Roche). If you've achieved all you've planned for yourself, you've not planned enough.

The desire for safety stands against every great and virtuous dream. Security is the first step toward stagnation. The trouble with this world is that too many people try to go through life with a catcher's mitt on both hands.

Boldness in vision is the first, second, and third most important thing. He who dares nothing should expect nothing. "One who is contented with what he has done will never be famous for what he will do" (Christian Bovee).

Be used for a mighty purpose. Martin Luther King Jr. said, "A man who won't die for something is not fit to live." Dare to do what's right for you. Choose a goal for which you are willing to exchange a piece of your life. The surest way to happiness is to lose yourself in a cause greater than you. You'll be unhappy if you don't reach for something beyond yourself.

"It is difficult to say what is impossible, for the dream of yesterday is the hope of today and the reality of tomorrow" (Robert Goddard). Reality is something you can rise above. Every great action is impossible when it is undertaken. Only after it has become accomplished does it seem possible to the average man. To small thinkers everything looks like a mountain. The grandest things are, in some ways, the easiest to do because there is so little competition.

To be complacently satisfied with yourself is a sure sign progress is about to end. If you're satisfied with yourself, you'd better change your ideals. "How much better to know that we have dared to live our dreams than to live our lives in a lethargy of regret" (Gilbert Caplin).

> Moderation is a fatal thing. Nothing succeeds like excess.
>
> Oscar Wilde

You'll never succeed beyond your wildest dreams . . . unless you have some wild dreams.

Do Today What
You Want to Postpone
until Tomorrow

The devil's favorite strategy to get you to fail is procrastination. Realize now is the best time to be alive and productive. If you want to make an easy job seem difficult, just keep putting off doing it. "We're all fugitives, and the things we didn't do yesterday are the bloodhounds" (*Prism*). "A duty dodged is like a debt unpaid; it is only deferred and we must come back and settle the account at last" (Joseph Newton). Work is the best thing ever invented for killing time.

What holds us back? "There are those of us who are always about to live. We're waiting until things change, until there is more time, until we are less tired, until we get a promotion, until we settle down—until, until, until. It always seems there is some major event that must occur in our lives before we begin living" (George Sheehan). *One* of these days is really *none* of these days. The by and by never comes. The person who desires but doesn't act breeds stagnation. And you should always expect poison from standing water.

About the only thing that comes to those who wait is old age. You can't build your reputation on what you're going to do tomorrow. Do today what you want to postpone until tomorrow. "Do not allow idleness to deceive you; for while you give him today, he steals tomorrow from you" (H. Crowquill). Nothing is so fatiguing as the eternal hanging-on of an uncompleted task. When you run in place, everyone will pass you by.

When people get into a habit of wasting time, they are sure to waste a great deal that doesn't belong to them. "One day, today, is worth two tomorrows" (Ben Franklin). What may be done at anytime . . . will be done at no time. "Life is like a taxi, the meter keeps a-ticking whether you're getting somewhere or standing still" (Lou Erickson). The successful person is someone who went ahead and did the things others never got around to.

A mother repeatedly called upstairs for her son to get up, get dressed, and get ready for school. It was a familiar routine, especially at exam time.

"I feel sick," said the voice from the bedroom.

"You are not sick. Get up and get ready," called the mother, walking up the stairs and hovering outside the bedroom door.

"I hate school and I'm not going," said the voice from the bedroom. "I'm always getting talked about behind my back, making mistakes, and getting told off. Nobody likes me, and I've got no friends. And we have too many tests. It's all just pointless, and I'm not going to school ever again."

"I'm sorry, but you are going to school," said the mother through the door, continuing encouragingly. "Really, mistakes are how we learn and develop. And please try not to take criticism so personally. And I can't believe that nobody likes you—you have lots of friends at school. And yes, all those tests can be daunting, but we are all tested in many ways throughout our lives, so all of this experience at school is useful for life in general. Besides, you have to go—you are the principal."

What the fool does in the end, the wise man does in the beginning. Prolonged idleness paralyzes initiative. "Don't stand shivering upon the banks; plunge in at once and have it over with" (Sam Slick). Tomorrow is the busiest day of the week. If there's a hill to climb, don't think waiting will make it any smaller.

A sluggard takes a hundred steps because he wouldn't take one in due time. If possible, make the decision now, even if the action is in the future. A reviewed decision is usually better than one reached at the last moment. "The fool with all his other thoughts, has this also; he is always getting ready to live" (Epicurus).

He who fiddles around seldom gets to lead the orchestra. There is danger in delay. It's always better to reap two days too soon than one day too late. Pity the man who waits until the last day.

"Tomorrow I will live," the fool does say; tomorrow itself is too late; the wise live yesterday.

Martial

While the fool is enjoying the little he has, I will hunt for more. The way to hunt for more is to utilize your odd moments. . . . The man who is always killing time is really killing his own chances in life.

Arthur Brisbane

Your Best Friends
Are Those Who Bring
Out the Best in You

Tell me who your best friends are, and I will tell you who you are. If you run with wolves, you will learn how to howl, but if you associate with eagles, you will learn how to soar to great heights. Proverbs 27:19 (TLB) says, "A mirror reflects a man's face, but what he is really like is shown by the kind of friends he chooses." The simple but true fact of life is that you become like those with whom you closely associate—for the good and the bad. Think about it; almost all of our sorrows spring out of relationships with the wrong people. Instead,

Keep out of the suction caused by those who drift backwards.

E. K. Piper

The less you associate with some people, the more your life will improve. Any time you indulge mediocrity in others it increases your mediocrity. A Bulgarian proverb confirms, "If you find yourself taking two steps forward and one step backwards, invariably it's because you have mixed associations in your life." If a loafer isn't a nuisance to you, it's a sign that you are somewhat of a loafer yourself. I have discovered that an important attribute in successful people is their impatience with people who think and act negatively. Misery wants your company. But you don't have to let it in the door. Proverbs 13:20 tells us,

> He that walketh with wise men shall be wise; but a companion of fools shall be destroyed.

We become like those with whom we associate.

We need to be careful of the kind of insulation we use in our lives. We do need to insulate ourselves from negative people and ideas, but we should never insulate ourselves from godly counsel and wisdom.

A number of years ago I found myself at a stagnation point in my life; I was unproductive and unable to see God's direction clearly. One day I noticed that almost all of my friends were in the same situation. When we got together, our problems were what we talked about. As I prayed about this matter, God showed me that I needed "foundation-level" people in my life. Such individuals bring out the best in us and influence us to improve. They cause us to have greater faith and confidence and to see things from God's perspective. After being with them, our spirits and our sights are raised.

The Lord showed me that I needed to change my closest associations and that I needed to have contact with the right people on a regular basis. These were men of strong faith, people who made me a better person when I was around them. They were the ones who saw the gifts in me and could correct me in a constructive, loving way. My choice to change my closest associations was a turning point in my life.

I have found that it is better to be alone than in the wrong company. A single conversation with the right person can be more valuable than years of study.

When you surround yourself with the right kind of people, you enter into the God-ordained power of agreement. Ecclesiastes 4:9–10, 12 (TLB) states,

> Two can accomplish more than twice as much as one, for the results can be much better. If one falls, the other pulls him up; but if a man falls when he is alone, he's in trouble. . . . And one standing alone can be attacked and defeated, but two can stand back-to-back and conquer; three is even better, for a triple-braided cord is not easily broken.

Steer clear of negative-thinking experts. Remember: In the eyes of average people, average is always considered outstanding. Look carefully at your closest associations, because it's an indication of the direction you're heading.

Always Say Less
Than You Know

Recently I saw a sign under a mounted largemouth bass: "If I had kept my mouth shut I wouldn't be here." How true! Don't jump into trouble mouth-first.

What we say is important. The book of Job reminds us, "How forcible are right words." Let me pose this question for you: What would happen if you changed what you said about your biggest problem, your biggest opportunity?

Our daily commitment ought to be, "Oh, please, fill my mouth with worthwhile stuff, and nudge me when I've said enough." The human tongue is only a few inches from the brain, but when you listen to some people talk, mouth and mind seem miles apart. The tongue runs fastest when the brain is in neutral.

A high school track coach was having difficulty motivating his athletes to perform at their best. The team had developed the distinctive reputation of coming in last at every meet they entered. One factor contributing to the coach's less-than-successful program was his pep-talk tactic. His most effective inspiring tool, he thought, was to tell his team, "Keep turning left and hurry back." Would that motivate you? Remember: Your words have the power to start fires or quench passion.

We should not be like the man who joined a monastery in which the monks were allowed to speak only two words every seven years. After the first seven years had passed, the "new" initiate met with the abbot, who asked him, "Well, what are your two words?"

"Food's bad," replied the man, who then went back to his silence.

Seven years later the clergyman asked, "What are your two words now?"

"Bed's hard," the man responded.

Seven years later—twenty-one years after his initial entry into the monastery—the man met with the abbot for the third and final time. "And what are your two words this time?" the abbot asked.

"I quit."

"Well, I'm not surprised," the cleric answered disgustedly. "All you've done since you got here is complain!"

Don't be known as a person whose only words are negative. Choose to speak positive, motivating, pleasant words. Blaise Pascal commented,

> Kind words do not cost much. They never blister the tongue or lips. Mental trouble was never known to arise from such quarters. Though they do not cost much, yet they accomplish much. They bring out a good nature in others. They also produce their own image on a man's soul, and what a beautiful image it is.

Sir Wilfred Grenfell said, "Start some kind word on its travels. There is no telling where the good it may do will stop."

> The words "I am . . ." are potent words; be careful what you hitch them to. The thing you're claiming has a way of reaching back and claiming you.
>
> A. L. Kitselman

Sometimes your biggest enemies and most trustworthy friends are the words you say to yourself. As Proverbs says, "Life and death are in the power of the tongue."

Henry Ward Beecher reflected,

> A helping word to one in trouble is often like the switch on a railroad track . . . an inch between a wreck and smooth rolling prosperity.

Johann Lavater advised, "Never tell evil of a man if you do not know it for certain, and if you know it for certain, then ask yourself, 'Why should I tell it?'"

What words have the most powerful effect on you? George Burnham said, "'I can't do it' never accomplished anything. 'I will try' has performed wonders."

> If your lips would keep from slips:
>   Five things observe with care;
>   To whom you speak, of whom you
>   speak,
>   And how, and when, and where.
>   Anonymous

Broken Promises Cause the World's Greatest Accidents

You can't make wrong work. Thomas Jefferson stated, "Honesty is the first chapter of the book of wisdom." Never chase a lie: If you leave it alone, it will run itself to death. Everything you add to the truth, you inevitably subtract from it. It's discouraging to think how people nowadays are more shocked by honesty than by deceit.

> Those that think it is permissible to tell "white lies" soon grow color-blind.
>
> Awson O'Malley

We punish ourselves with every lie, and we reward ourselves with every right action. A lie will add to your troubles, subtract from your energy, multiply your difficulties, and divide your effectiveness.

> Truth is always strong, no matter how weak it looks, and falsehood is always weak no matter how strong it looks.
>
> Marcus Antonius

Never view anything positively that makes you break your word. Make your word your bond.

In the war between falsehood and truth, falsehood may win the first battle, but truth wins the war. "If we live truly, we shall truly live," said Ralph Waldo Emerson. Liars are never free. Horace Greeley observed,

> The darkest hour of any man's life is when he sits down to plan how to get money without earning it.

The book of Proverbs says it best: "Dishonest gain will never last, so why take the risk?" Honesty always lasts longest. A lie never lives to be old.

"It makes all the difference in the world whether we put truth in the first place or in the second place" (John Morley). As scarce as the truth is, the supply has always been in excess of the demand. Wrong is wrong no matter who does it or says it. Truth does not cease to exist because it is ignored, and it doesn't change depending on whether it is believed by a majority. The truth is always the strongest argument.

Truth exists; only lies are created. Truth shines in darkness:

> There is never an instant's truth between virtue and vice. Goodness is the only investment that never fails.
>
> Henry David Thoreau

Truth needs no crutches. If it limps, it's a lie. "You'll find that life is an uphill battle for the person who's not on the level" (Joan Welsh).

"If you continue to do what's right, what's wrong and who's wrong will eventually leave your life" (David Blunt). One businessman had a personalized letterhead that read, "Right is right even if everyone is against it, and wrong is wrong even if everyone is for it."

Consider the words of John Wesley:

> Do all the good you can,
>> In all the ways you can,
>>> In all the places you can,
> At all times you can,
>> To all the people you can,
>>> As long as ever you can.

You Can't Get Ahead
When You're Trying
to Get Even

Never cut what can be untied.

Joseph Joubert

When you have been wronged, a poor memory is your best response. Never carry a grudge. While you're straining under its weight, the person with whom you're mad is out producing.

Forgive your enemies—nothing annoys them more. There is no revenge so sweet as forgiveness. The only people you should try to get even with are those who have helped you.

"Forgiveness ought to be like a canceled note—torn in two, and burned up, so that it never can be shown against one" (Henry Ward Beecher). One of the greatest strengths you can display is forgoing revenge and daring to forgive an injury.

> He who cannot forgive destroys the bridge over which he may one day need to pass.
>
> Larry Bielat

The one guaranteed formula for limiting your potential is unforgiveness. Hate, bitterness, and revenge are luxuries you cannot afford.

People need loving most when they deserve it least. Forgiveness heals; unforgiveness wounds. When we think about offenses, trouble grows; when we forgive, trouble goes.

Our forgiveness for others brings assurance of God's forgiveness for us. In Matthew 6:14–15 (NIV), Jesus said,

> If you forgive other people when they sin against you, your heavenly Father will also

forgive you. But if you do not forgive others their sins, your Father will not forgive your sins.

The weight of unforgiveness greatly drags a person down. It is a tremendous load to carry in the race we're called to run.

When faced with the need to forgive and forget, never make the excuse, "But you don't know what he/she did to me!" That may be true, but it's more important to know what unforgiveness will do to you.

What really matters is what happens *in* us, not *to* us. Unforgiveness leads to great bitterness, which is a deadly misuse of the creative flow from above. Great amounts of brainpower are used up when you ponder a negative situation and plot how to get even. This kind of thinking is completely unproductive. People who burn bridges will be isolated and alone and will deal with neutrals and enemies the rest of their lives. That's why we should build bridges, not burn them.

Vengeance is a poor traveling companion. Every Christian is called to a ministry of reconciliation (2 Cor. 5:18). Getting even always causes imbalance and unhappiness.

When you don't forgive, you are ignoring its impact on your destiny:

> Hate is a prolonged form of suicide.
>
> Douglas V. Steere

How much more grievous are the consequences of unforgiveness than the causes of it! Norman Cousins summed it up when he said, "Life is an adventure in forgiveness."

It's true that the one who forgives ends the quarrel. Patting a fellow on the back is the best way to get a chip off his shoulder. Forgive your enemies—you can't get back at them any other way!

Forgiveness saves the expense of anger, the high cost of hatred, and the waste of energy. There are two marks of greatness: giving and forgiving.

If you want to be miserable, hate somebody.
Unforgiveness does a great deal more damage
to the vessel in which it is stored than the object
on which it is poured.

Every person should have a special cemetery
lot in which to bury the faults of friends and
loved ones. To forgive is to set a prisoner free
and discover the prisoner was you.

Unknown

The Most Natural Thing to Do When You Get Knocked Down Is to Get Back Up

There is no overestimating how we respond to failures and mistakes. How do *you* respond to failure? Failure does not mean that nothing has been accomplished. There is *always* the opportunity to learn something.

We all experience failure and make mistakes. In fact, successful people have more failure in their lives than average people do. Great people throughout history have all failed at some point. Those who do not expect anything are never disappointed; those who never try, never fail. Anyone who is currently achieving anything in life is simultaneously risking failure. It is always better to fail in doing something than to excel at doing nothing. A flawed diamond is more valuable than a perfect brick. People who have no failures also have few victories.

People get knocked down; it is how fast they get up that counts. As we have seen, there is a positive correlation between spiritual maturity and how quickly a person responds to failures and mistakes. Individuals who are spiritually mature have a greater ability to get up and go on than people who are spiritually immature. The less developed the person, the longer he holds on to past failures. God never sees us as failures; He only sees us as learners.

Paul Galvin, at the age of thirty-three, had twice failed in enterprise. Then he attended an auction of his own storage-battery business and, with his last $750, bought back the battery-eliminator portion of it. This part became Motorola. Upon his retirement in the 1960s, he advised, "Do not fear mistakes. You will know failure. Continue to reach out." To expect your life to be perfectly tailored to your specifications is to live a life of continual frustration.

David McNally mused, "The mistake-riddled life is much richer, more interesting, and more stimulating than the life that has never risked or taken a stand on anything." What is the difference between the champion and the average person? Tom Hopkins says,

> The single most important difference between champion achievers and average people is their ability to handle rejection and failure.

Listen to S. I. Hayakawa:

> Notice the difference between what happens when a man says to himself, "I failed three times," than what happens when he says, "I am a failure."

Failure is a situation, never a person.

You can't travel the road to success without a puncture or two. Mistakes are often the best teachers. Ecclesiastes advises, "In the day of prosperity be joyful, but in the day of adversity consider." Oswald Avery says, "Whenever you fall, pick something up." The man who invented the eraser had the human race pretty well figured out. You will find that people who never make mistakes don't make much else. You can profit from your errors.

Failure is not falling down but staying down. Be like Jonah, who, when swallowed by a large fish, proved that you can't keep a good man under water. Remember that a stumble is not a fall—in fact, a stumble may actually prevent a fall. Herman Melville wrote, "He who has never failed somewhere, that man cannot be great."

Not remembered for his failures but for his successes, inventor Thomas Edison reflected,

> People are not remembered by how few times they failed, but by how often they succeed. Every wrong step can be another step forward.

David Burns said, "Assert your right to make a few mistakes. If people can't accept your imperfection, that's their fault." Robert Schuller wrote, "Look at what you have left, never look at what you have lost." If you learn from them, mistakes are invaluable. Cultivate this attitude and you will never be ashamed to try.

We truly fail only when we do not learn from an experience. The decision is up to us. We can choose to turn a failure into either a hitching post or a guidepost.

Here is the key to being free from the stranglehold of past failures and mistakes: Learn the lesson and forget the details. Have you ever noticed that the devil never reminds you of the lesson? He only wants you to remember the details. Gain from the experience, but do not roll the minute details of it over and over in your mind. Build on the lesson, and get on with your life.

Remember that the call is higher than the fall.

Part Three

LOOKING UPWARD

You Can Never Trust God Too Much

Many people believe in God, but not many *believe God*. One of the most incredible places we can live our lives is in a continual position of believing God. "God made us, and God is able to empower us to do whatever He calls us to do. Denying we can accomplish God's work is not humility; it is the worst kind of pride" (Warren Wiersbe).

The person who puts God first will find God with him right up to the last. "In everything you do, put God first, and he will direct you and crown your efforts with success" (Prov. 3:6 TLB). Unless it includes trusting God, it's not worthy of being called His direction. Every divine direction we receive from God includes Him.

181

"God never made a promise that was too good to be true" (D. L. Moody). One of the great things about believing God is found in Luke 18:27, where Jesus says, "The things which are impossible with men are possible with God." When you join together with Him in His plan, things that were impossible now become possible. The superior person seeks success in God. The small person seeks success in self. You've never tapped God's resources until you have attempted the impossible.

You may trust the Lord too little, but you can never trust Him too much. With His strength behind you, His love with you, and His arms underneath you, you are more than sufficient for the days ahead of you.

> I trust that God is on our side. But, it is more important to know that we are on God's side.
>
> Abraham Lincoln

The fact is, anyone who doesn't believe in miracles is not a realist. Look around—nothing is more real than miracles. When you leave God out, you'll find yourself without any *invisible* means of support. Nothing great has been achieved except by those who dared believe God inside them was superior to any circumstance.

To say "impossible" always puts you on the losing side. If you dream big, believe big, and pray big, do you know what happens? Big things! Most of the things worth doing in history were declared impossible before they were done. What's possible is our highest responsibility.

If you put a buzzard in a pen six or eight feet square and entirely open at the top, the bird, in spite of his ability to fly, will be an absolute prisoner. The reason is that a buzzard always begins a flight from the ground with a run of ten or twelve feet. Without space to run, as is his habit, he will not even attempt to fly but will remain a prisoner for life in a small jail with no top.

If dropped into an open tumbler, a bumble-bee will be there until it dies unless it is taken out. It never sees the means of escape at the top but persists in trying to find some way out through the sides near the bottom. It will seek a way where none exists until it completely destroys itself.

Don't be like the buzzard and the bee, struggling with problems and frustrations, not realizing your answer is right there above you.

The way each day will look to you all starts with *whom* you're looking to. Look to God. Believe God. When you believe God you will see an opportunity in every problem, not problems in the middle of every opportunity. Proverbs 16:3 is true when it says, "Commit to the LORD whatever you do, and he will establish your plans" (NIV). Joshua 1:9 also says, "Yes, be bold and strong! Banish fear and doubt! For remember, the Lord your God is with you wherever you go" (TLB).

All great things have God involved in them. Dare to go with God farther than you can see right now. If something is beneficial for you, God will put it within your reach. One psalm in the Bible says, "No good thing will he with-hold from them that walk uprightly" (Ps. 84:11). Never undertake anything for which you wouldn't have the conviction to ask the blessing of heaven. A small person stands on others. A great person stands with God.

Destiny Delayed Is the Devil's Delight

The most important moment in your life is right now. Don't let hesitation and procrastination keep you from your destiny. Procrastination is the symptom, fear is the problem. When you delay your duties, you delight the devil.

Be jealous of your time; it's your greatest treasure. Ideas have a short shelf life—that's why we must act before the expiration date. Procrastination is the "skill" of keeping up with yesterday.

> Even if you're on the right track—you'll get run over if you just sit there.
>
> Arthur Goodfrey

Putting off a simple thing makes it hard, and putting off a hard thing makes it impossible. Discouragement follows any decision to avoid a priority.

Obedience is God's method of provision for your life. Isaiah reminds us, "If ye be willing and obedient, ye shall eat the good of the land" (1:19). Faith triggers divine resources when you go where God leads you. Obedience brings blessings. Delayed obedience is disobedience. Obedience means "at once."

Today is the day to start. It's always too soon to stop. Many times we're not to understand, just obey. The quickest way to get out of the hole is to obey God. There's a reason God revealed the idea to you today. Peter urges, "We ought to obey God rather than men" (Acts 5:29). Choosing to obey men is what keeps us from being quick to obey God. What we all need is an alarm clock that rings when it's time to rise to the occasion.

Why don't we jump at opportunities as quickly as we jump to conclusions? Procrastination is the grave in which opportunity is buried. Anybody who brags about what he's going to do tomorrow probably did the same thing yesterday. Few things are more dangerous to a person's character than having nothing to do and plenty of time in which to do it. Killing time is not murder, it's suicide. Two things rob people of their peace of mind: work unfinished and work not yet begun.

Opportunity is often lost by deliberation. Charles Sheldon once said, "Good resolutions are like babies crying in church: They should be carried out immediately." Tackle any challenge at first sight; the longer you stare at it, the bigger it becomes. The lazier a man is, the more he's going to do tomorrow. The tragedy of life is not that it ends so soon, but that we wait so long to begin it.

The longer it takes to act on God's direction, the more unclear the direction will become. Be quick to obey, taking action without delay.

Once upon a time, the devil decided to destroy humankind. He called in all his little devils to make the plans. Anger came first and asked to be allowed to do the job by setting brother against brother. He would make people angry with each other and they would destroy themselves.

Lust also offered to go. He would defile minds and turn people into beasts by making love disappear. Next, Greed spoke and offered to destroy humankind with the most destructive of passions: uncontrolled desires. Idleness, Hate, Jealousy, and Envy each claimed in turn that they could do the job. But the devil was not satisfied with any one of them.

Finally, the last assistant came forward. He said, "I will talk with people persuasively in terms of all that God wants them to be. I shall tell them how fine their plans are to be honest, clean, and brave. I shall encourage them in the good purposes of life!"

The devil was aghast at such talk. But then the assistant continued, "I shall tell them there is no hurry. They can do all of these things tomorrow. I shall advise them to wait until conditions become more favorable before they start!" The devil replied, "You are the one who shall go to earth to destroy humankind!" The assistant's name was Procrastination.

There Are No Unimportant People

You're not insignificant. Never view your life as if Jesus did nothing for you. Make the most of yourself; that's exactly how God made you. Even a small star shines in the darkness from millions of miles away. The first and worst of all frauds is to limit oneself.

Too many people never begin what God wants them to do because they are waiting to sing like Sandi Patti, preach like Billy Graham, or write like Max Lucado. God knew what He was doing when He put you together. Use what talents *you* possess . . . the woods would be silent if the only birds singing were those that sang the best.

"All history is a record of the power of minorities, and of minorities of one" (Ralph

Waldo Emerson). If you deliberately plan to be less than you're capable of being, you'll be frustrated for the rest of your life.

View others in this same light. Each person is valuable and precious. Each person knows something you don't. Learn from them. We're all created for achievement and given the seeds for greatness, but each in our own way. What is greatness? What is achievement? Doing what God wants you to do and being where He wants you to be. There are no unimportant people.

Christians are new creations, not resurfaced sinners. With God's help, you can be one of His few successes, not one of His thousands of disappointments. Don't ever forget that God calls you a friend (see John 15:13). What an incredible statement that is! He also says you're "fearfully and wonderfully made" (Ps. 139:14).

God made you special for a purpose. He has an assignment for you that no one else can do as well as you can. Out of billions of applicants for the job, you're the most qualified. You have the right combination of what it takes. God has given each person the measure of faith to do what He's called them to do. Every person is gifted.

You are never who you ought to be until you are doing what you ought to be doing. God holds us responsible not only for what we have, but for what we could have; not only for who we are, but for who we might be. People are responsible to God for becoming what God has made possible for them to become.

Your life makes a difference. Although we're all different, no mixture is insignificant. On judgment day, God won't ask me why I wasn't Joshua, Billy Graham, or Pat Robertson . . . but why I wasn't John Mason. Jerry Van Dyke said it best: "The best rose bush is not the one with the fewest thorns, but that which bears the finest roses."

Few Dreams Come True by Themselves; the Test of a Person Lies in Action

No one ever stumbled onto something big while sitting down. Even a mosquito doesn't get a slap on the back until it starts to work. A famous anonymous poem states,

> Sitting still and wishing makes no
> person great,
> The good Lord sends the fishing, but
> you must dig the bait.

"As [Jesus] was speaking, a woman in the crowd called out, 'God bless your mother—the womb from which you came, and the breasts that gave you suck!' He replied, 'Yes, but even more blessed are all who hear the Word of God and put it into practice'" (Luke 11:27–28 TLB). A doer of God's Word is even more blessed than the mother of Jesus.

Realize nothing is learned while you talk. Words without actions are the assassins of dreams. The smallest good deed is better than the greatest intention. History is made whenever you take the right action. Action is the proper fruit of knowledge. Getting an idea should be like sitting on a tack: it should make you jump up and do something.

"Go to the ant, thou sluggard; consider her ways, and be wise: which having no guide, overseer, or ruler, providing her meat in the summer, and gathereth her food in the harvest" (Prov. 6:6–8). Nothing preaches better than an ant, even though it says nothing. You earn respect by action; inaction earns disrespect.

You should hunt for the good points in people. Remember, they have to do the same in your case . . . so do something to help them.

A middle-aged man found himself in front of the pearly gates. St. Peter explained that it's not so easy to get into heaven. There are some criteria before entry is allowed.

St. Peter asked if the man was religious in life. Did he attend church? The man answered, "No." St. Peter told him that was bad.

Was he generous? Did he give money to the poor or to charities? Again the answer was "No." St. Peter told him that was not good.

Did he do any good deeds? Help his neighbor? Anything? Still, his answer was "No." St. Peter was becoming concerned.

Exasperated, Peter said, "Look, everybody does something nice sometime. Work with me, I'm trying to help. Now think!"

The man paused and said, "There was this old lady. I came out of a store and found her surrounded by a dozen Hell's Angels. They had taken her purse and were shoving her around, taunting and cursing her.

"I got so mad I threw my bags down, fought through the crowd, and got her purse back. I helped her to her feet. I then went up to the biggest, baddest biker and told him how despicable, cowardly, and mean he was and then spat in his face."

"Wow!" said Peter. "That's impressive. When did this happen?"

"Oh, about two minutes ago," replied the man.

Some people find life an empty dream because they put nothing into it. Every time one person expresses an idea, you can find ten others who thought of it before—but took no action. Mark Twain once said, "Thunder is good, thunder is impressive, but it is lightning that does the work." The test of this book is not the reader saying "What an inspiring book!" but "I will do something!"

The devil is willing for you to confess faith as long as you don't practice it. When praying, we must simultaneously be willing to take the action God directs in the answer to our prayer. The answers to your prayers will include action. Action is attached to answers and miracles.

The Bible tells us action gives life to our faith (see James 2:26). "Even a child is known by his doings" (Prov. 20:11). Many churchgoers are singing "Standing on the Promises" when all they are doing is sitting on the premises. Too many people carefully avoid discovering the secret of success because deep down they suspect the secret may be hard work.

Adopt the Pace of God

God is a planner, a strategist. He is perfectly organized, has a definite flow and pace. God is more like a marathon runner than a sprinter. He has our whole lives in mind, not just tomorrow. Remember, God is never late. Never try to hurry God. "He that believeth shall not make haste" (Isa. 28:16). Urgent matters are seldom urgent. Pressure usually accompanies us when we are out of God's pace.

Proverbs 16:9 says, "We should make plans—counting on God to direct us" (TLB). And Proverbs 16:3 tells us, "Commit to the LORD whatever you do, and he will establish your plans" (NIV). Those who are lukewarm give up along the way, and cowards never even start. God is the original's hope but the copy's excuse. Is God your hope or your excuse?

Adopt the pace of God. His secret is patience. There's no time lost in waiting if you're waiting on the Lord . . . and He's worth your time. The road to success runs uphill, so don't expect to break any speed records. All great achievements require time. Happiness is a direction, not a destination.

During the darkest hours of the Civil War, Abraham Lincoln responded to the question of whether he was sure God was on the North's side: "I do not know: I have not thought about that. But I am very anxious to know whether we are on God's side." Lincoln's contemporary, Henry Ward Beecher, once said, "The strength of a man consists in finding out the way God is going, and going that way."

Walking at God's pace helps establish you on the proper foundation. Nothing is permanent unless built on God's will and Word. "Except the LORD build the house, they labour in vain that build it" (Ps. 127:1). "The steps of a good man are ordered by the LORD: and he delighteth in his way" (Ps. 37:23). Never remain where

God has not sent you. When God shuts and bolts the door, don't try to get in through the window.

A Christian walking in God's pace is like a candle—it must keep cool and burn at the same time. (But if you burn the candle at both ends, you're not as bright as you think.)

Every great person first learned how to obey, whom to obey, and when to obey.

> The place I choose, or place I shun,
> My soul is satisfied with none;
> But when Thy will directs my way,
> Tis equal joy to go or stay.
>
> Anonymous

In the Race for Excellence, There Is No Finish Line

Commit yourself to excellence from the start. No legacy is as rich as excellence. The quality of your life will be in direct proportion to your commitment to excellence, regardless of what you choose to do.

> It's a fun thing about life; if you refuse to accept anything but the best, you very often get it.
>
> Somerset Maugham

It takes less time to do something right than it does to explain why you did it wrong. According to Orison Swett Marden, "There is an infinite difference between a little wrong and just right, between fairly good and the best, between mediocrity and superiority." Every day you should ask yourself: Why should my boss/client hire me instead of someone else? Why should people do business with me instead of my competitors?

> Watch your actions; they become habits. Watch your habits; they become character. Watch your character; it becomes your destiny.
>
> Frank Outlaw

Oliver Wendell Holmes once said, "Sin has many tools, but a lie is the handle that fits them all." Those who are given to telling white lies soon become color blind. You may go to the ends of the earth by lying, but you'll never get back. A lie has no legs to support itself—it requires other lies. When you stretch the truth, watch out for the snap back. Each time you lie, even just a little white lie, you push yourself toward failure. There is no right way to do the wrong thing. Each time you're honest you propel yourself toward greater success.

Reputation grows like a mushroom; character grows like an oak tree. A thing done right means less trouble tomorrow. Beware of a half-truth; you may get hold of the wrong half. Only you can damage your character. People of genius are admired; people of wealth are envied; people of power are feared; but only people of character are trusted.

Outside forces don't control your character. You do. The measure of your real character is what you would do if you knew you would never be found out. Be more concerned with your character than with your reputation, because your character is what you really are while your reputation is merely what others think you are.

He that is good will infallibly become better, and he that is bad, will as certainly become worse; for vice, virtue and time are three things that never stand still.

Charles Caleb Colton

Excellence can be attained if you . . .
Care more than others think is wise.
Risk more than others think is safe.
Dream more than others think is
    practical.
Expect more than others think is
    possible.

                            Anonymous

Is God Finished with You Yet?

If you're still breathing, the answer is no. Don't die until you're dead. Psalm 138:8 says, "The LORD will perfect that which concerneth me." God is continually perfecting and fine-tuning each of us. He wants to fulfill all of His promises and purposes in our lives.

Romans 11:29 says, "For God's gifts and his call are irrevocable" (NIV). What God has put in you stays your whole life. He still wants to use what He's given in order to fulfill His plan for your life. If you've done nothing with what He's put inside of you . . . He still wants to use you! If you've failed many times . . . He still wants to use you! How do you move again with God? Say this simple prayer: "Lord, send small opportunities into my life so I can begin to use what You've put inside of me."

Ralph Waldo Emerson said, "The creation of a thousand forests is in one acorn." The accomplishment of your destiny is held in the seeds of your God-given gifts and calling.

God begins with a positive and ends with a positive. "Being confident of this very thing, that he which hath begun a good work in you will perform it until the day of Jesus Christ" (Phil. 1:6). Jesus hasn't come back, so that means God isn't finished with you. God's will for us is momentum, building from one good work to another.

Don't just go on to other things, go on to higher things. The pains of being a Christian are all growing pains, and those growing pains lead to maturity. God's way becomes plain as we walk in it. When faith is stretched, it grows. "The more we do, the more we can do" (William Hazlitt).

Greater opportunity and momentum is the reward of past accomplishment. If you're going to climb, you've got to grab the branches, not the blossoms. Success makes failures out of too many people when they stop after a victory. Don't quit. Don't stop after a victory. When you do what you can, God will do what you can't. He's not finished with you!

Once You've Found a Better Way, Make That Way Better

All progress is due to those who weren't satisfied to let well enough alone. "Acorns were good until bread was found" (Francis Bacon). The majority of people meet with failure because they lack persistence in creating new plans to add to those that succeed.

If at first you do succeed, try something harder. There's no mistake as great as the mistake of not going on after a victory. If you can't think up a new idea, find a way to make better use of an old one. "Where we cannot invent, we may at least improve" (Charles Caleb Colton).

Don't look for *the* answer to your problem; look for *many* answers, then choose the best one.

The person who succeeds is the one who does more than is necessary—and continues doing it. As Zig Ziglar says, "The difference between ordinary and extraordinary is that little extra."

There's always a way, and there's always a better way. When you've found something—look again. School is never out! The more you truly desire something, the more you will try to find a better way.

The deeper we go in God, the deeper He goes in us. "A wise man will hear, and will increase learning" (Prov. 1:5). If you're satisfied with what's good, you'll never have what's best.

"It's what you learn after you know it all that counts" (John Wooden). The man who thinks he knows it all has merely stopped thinking. If you think you've arrived, you'll be left behind. The important thing is this: to be able at any moment to sacrifice what we are for what we could become. A successful person continues to look for work even after he has found a job.

Cause something to happen. Thomas Edison said, "Show me a thoroughly satisfied man, I will show you a failure." "There are two kinds of men who never amount to very much," Cyrus H. K. Curtis remarked one day to his associate, Edward Bok. "And what kinds are those?" inquired Bok. "Those who cannot do what they are told," replied the famous publisher, "and those who can do nothing else." Find a better way and make that better.

The Doors of Opportunity Are Marked "Push"

Get aggressive and go after opportunities. Otherwise, they may not find you. The reason some people don't go very far in life is because they sidestep opportunity and shake hands with procrastination. Procrastination is the grave in which opportunity is buried. When opportunity knocks at your front door, don't be caught out in the backyard looking for four-leaf clovers. For the tenacious person there is always time and opportunity.

Watch for big problems; they disguise big opportunities. Opposition, distraction, and challenges always surround the birth of a dream.

So make the most of all that comes and the least of all that goes. Adversity is fertile soil for creativity.

To the alert Christian, interruptions are divinely inserted opportunities. If you're looking for a big opportunity, look for a big problem. Turn the tables on adversity. Adversity has advantages.

Life's disappointments are opportunity's hidden appointments. When God is going to do something wonderful, He begins with difficulty; when He's going to do something very wonderful, He begins with impossibility!

Francis Bacon said, "A wise man will make more opportunities than he finds." It's more valuable to find a situation that redistributes opportunity than one that redistributes wealth. Have you ever noticed that great people are never lacking for opportunities? When highly successful people are interviewed, they always mention their big plans for the future. Most of us would think, "If I were in their shoes, I'd kick back and do nothing." Success doesn't diminish their dreams. They've always been that way, even before they were great.

There's far more opportunity than ability. Life's full of golden opportunities for doing what we're called to do. Start with what you can do; don't stop because of what you can't do. In the orchard of opportunity, it is better to pick the fruit than to wait for it to fall in your lap.

Greater opportunities and joy come to those who make the most of small opportunities. In the parable of the talents the master told the servant who used what he had, "Well done, good and faithful servant; thou hast been faithful over a few things, I will make thee ruler over many things: enter thou into the joy of thy Lord" (Matt. 25:23).

Many people seem to think opportunity means a chance to get money without earning it. God's best gifts to us are not things but opportunities. And those doors of opportunity are marked "Push."

Opportunity is all around you.

Count God's Blessings, Don't Discount Them

Be aggressively thankful. When it comes to living your life, an important issue is whether you take things for granted or take them with gratitude. Thanksgiving is an attitude of a productive life. No duty is more urgent than that of returning thanks. People who aren't thankful for what they've got aren't likely to be thankful for what they're going to get. Ingratitude never finishes.

"Attitudes sour in the life that is closed to thankfulness. Soon selfish attitudes take over, closing life to better things" (C. Neil Strait). The person who forgets the language of gratitude will never find herself on speaking terms with happiness. Thanksgiving, you will find, creates power in your life because it opens the generators of your heart to respond gratefully, to receive joyfully, and to react creatively.

> There are three enemies of personal peace: regret over yesterday's mistakes, anxiety over tomorrow's problems, and ingratitude for today's blessing.
>
> William Ward

Know you are blessed. If you can't be satisfied with what you've reached . . . at least be thankful for what you've escaped. I remember several years ago driving to dinner, completely absorbed in thought about my latest book. I was so focused, in fact, that I drove right through a red light at a major intersection in the city where I live. After being greeted by several horns and one man who wanted to let me know with his finger that I was "number one," I pulled into a parking lot and gave thanks to God for His protection . . . even when I'm stupid.

We all have a lot to be thankful for. We all have a lot to be thankful for!

Thank God and count your blessings at every opportunity. The words *think* and *thank* come from the same Latin root. If we take time to think more we will undoubtedly thank more. When you start to find fault with all you see, it is time to start looking for what's wrong with you.

I like what Dwight L. Moody said: "Be humble or you'll stumble." There's a connection between pride and ingratitude. Henry Ward Beecher pointed out, "A proud man is seldom a grateful man, for he never thinks he gets as much as he deserves." Don't be a person who has a highly developed instinct for being unhappy. Instead, "Be glad for all God is planning for you. Be patient in trouble, and prayerful always" (Rom. 12:12 TLB). The best rule is to gratefully receive whatever God gives. If we spend our time thanking God for the good things, there won't be any time left to complain about the bad.

Take some time today and sincerely consider how many things you have to be thankful for.

Consider writing them down and keeping that list easily available to you. As you do, I guarantee creative ideas will spring forth from the discussion you are having with yourself. One of the most creative ways to generate momentum and opportunities is to sit down and write a note, place a call, or send an email to say thank you to those people who have influenced your life. Try to do this for as many people as you genuinely can.

There's nothing worse the earth produces than an ungrateful person. Our real prosperity lies in being thankful. Appreciative words are the most powerful force for good on the earth. Kind words don't cost much, but yet they accomplish much.

Count God's blessings, don't discount them. Pray this prayer: "God, you've given so much to me. Give me one more thing—a grateful heart."

Be Easily Satisfied
with the Very Best

Start every task thinking how to do it better than it's ever been done before. "Start a crusade in your life to dare to be your very best" (William Danforth). Become a yardstick of quality. Do the right thing regardless of what others think. Most people aren't used to an environment where excellence is expected.

"It is a funny thing about life; if you refuse to accept anything but the best, you very often get it" (Somerset Maugham). Think only of the best, work only for the best, and expect only the best. Excellence is never an accident. "There is a way to do it better . . . find it" (Thomas Edison). There's always an excellent way of doing everything. "Hold yourself responsible for a higher standard than anybody else expects of you. Never excuse yourself" (Henry Ward Beecher).

> It is those who have this imperative demand for the best in their natures and those who will accept nothing short of it, that hold the banners of progress, that set the standards, the ideals for others.
>
> Orison Marden

> Happy is the man who doesn't give in and do wrong when he is tempted, for afterwards he will get as his reward the crown of life that God has promised those who love him.
>
> James 1:12 TLB

Excellence measures a person by the height of one's ideals, the breadth of one's compassion, the depth of one's convictions, and the length of one's persistence. People will always determine your character by observing what you stand for, fall for, or lie for.

Perfection, fortunately, is not the best alternative to mediocrity. A more sensible alternative is excellence. Striving for excellence rather than perfection is stimulating and rewarding; striving for absolute perfection—in practically anything—is frustrating and futile. We are what we repeatedly do. Excellence, then, is not an act but a habit.

"I advise you to obey only the Holy Spirit's instructions. He will tell you where to go and what to do, and then you won't always be doing the wrong things your evil nature wants you to do" (Gal. 5:16 TLB). Human excellence means nothing unless it works with the consent of God. "Excellence demands that you be better than yourself" (Ted Engstrom).

There's always a heavy demand for fresh mediocrity—don't give in to it. Instead, be easily satisfied with the very best. When you're delivering your very best, that's when you'll feel most successful.

Your character is your destiny. Never sell your principles for popularity or you'll find yourself bankrupt in the worst way. Dare to be true to the best you know.

If God Is Your Father,
Please Call Home

Prayer brings momentum. It lifts the heart above the challenges of life and gives it a view of God's resources of victory and hope. Prayer provides power, poise, peace, and purpose for a person's purpose, plans, and pursuits. The most powerful energy anyone can generate is prayer energy.

> The devil smiles when we make plans.
> He laughs when we get too busy.
> But he trembles when we pray.
>
> Corrie ten Boom

Don't worry about anything; instead, pray about everything; tell God your needs and don't forget to thank him for his answers. If you do this, you will experience God's peace, which is far more wonderful than the human mind can understand.

Philippians 4:6–7 TLB

Whatever is worth worrying about is certainly worth praying about. God is never more than a prayer away from you. When you feel swept off your feet, get back to your knees.

If I could hear Christ praying for me in the next room, I would not fear a million enemies. Yet distance makes no difference. He is praying for me.

Robert Murray McCheyne

Heaven is ready to receive you when you pray. "Time spent in communion with God is never lost" (Gordon Lindsay).

I have so much to do today that I shall spend the first three hours in prayer.

Martin Luther

223

Common people do not pray, they only beg. So pray, don't beg. When we pray, we link ourselves with God's inexhaustible power and insight. "Wishing will never be a substitute for prayer" (Edwin Louis Cole).

Remember that prayers can't be answered until they are prayed. "Whatever things you ask when you pray, believe that you receive them, and you will have them" (Mark 11:24 NKJV).

> A day hemmed in prayer is less likely to unravel.
>
> Anonymous

When we pray, we must simultaneously position ourselves to be willing to take the action that God requires as answers to our prayer because "prayer is not monologue but dialogue; God's voice in response to mine is its most essential part" (Andrew Murray). The prayers a person lives on his feet are no less important than those he says on his knees.

Practical prayer is harder on the soles of your shoes than on the knees of your trousers.

Osten O'Malley

The strongest action that you can take in any situation is to go to your knees and ask God for help. The highest purpose of faith or prayer is not to change my circumstances but to change me. Pray to do the will of God in every situation—nothing else is worth praying for.

Do not have your concert and tune your instruments afterwards. Begin the day with God.

James Hudson Taylor

Prayer may not change all things for you, but it sure changes you for all things. Prayer is the stop that keeps you going. If God is your Father, please call home.

The Worst Liars in
the World Are
Your Own Fears

It's never safe to look into the future with eyes of fear. "Worry is the traitor in our camp that dampens our powder and weakens our aim" (William Jorden).

> Worry is faith in the negative, trust in the unpleasant, assurance of disaster, and belief in defeat. . . . Worry is a magnet that attracts negative conditions. Faith is a more powerful force that creates positive circumstances. . . . Worry is wasting today's time to clutter up tomorrow's opportunities with yesterday's troubles.
>
> William A. Ward

Let him have all your worries and cares, for he is always thinking about you and watching everything that concerns you.

1 Peter 5:7 TLB

Never make a decision based on fear, and never fear to make a decision. Worry comes when human beings interfere with God's plan for their lives. Don't ever find yourself giving the "benefit of the doubt"—doubt has no benefit.

What causes most battles to be lost is the unfounded fear of the enemy's strength. Never look at your uncertain future with eyes of fear. A. Parnell Bailey says worry is like a fog:

The Bureau of Standards in Washington tells us a dense fog covering seven city blocks, one hundred feet deep, is composed of something less than one glass of water. That amount of water is divided into some 60,000,000 tiny drops. Not much there! Yet when these minute particles settle down over the city or countryside, they can blot out practically all vision. A cup full of worry does just about the same thing. We forget to trust God. The tiny drops of fretfulness close around our thoughts and we are submerged without vision.

Scott Williams shares this story:

Ron Wayne was one of the original Co-founders of Apple. Ron Wayne along with Steve Jobs "Jobs" and Steve Wozniak "Woz" were the original Apple Founding Trifecta. Wayne is actually responsible for designing the company's original logo. The Apple Logo has evolved into what we have come to know as the forbidden fruit that looks like Adam or Eve took a bite out of. Wayne also wrote the original Apple manual and drew up this start-up company's partnership agreement.

Wayne set himself up for financial success and the original agreement gave him a 10 percent ownership stake in Apple, a position that would be worth $22 billion dollars today if Wayne had held onto it. Instead of holding onto it, Wayne dropped it like it was hot. Ooops, Bad Move!

According to Mercury News, Wayne was afraid that Jobs' wild spending and Woz's life of bling before bling was bling would cause Apple to flop. Wayne decided to step down from his role of being the "mature one" in the bunch. Wayne took a bite out of the Apple and left the company after only 11 days. Wayne was a little more worried than Jobs or Woz because he was the only one of the three founders with assets that creditors could seize; he sold back his shares for $800. Let me repeat that last line . . . Wayne sold his shares for $800.

One of the best discoveries you can make is to find you *can* do what you were afraid you couldn't do. Fear and self-sabotage lock people's minds against fresh ideas. When you are ruled by fear, you'll find yourself unable to make the very changes that will eliminate it.

An old man was asked what had robbed him of joy in his life. His reply was, "Things that never happened." Do you remember the things you were worrying about a year ago?

How did they work out? Didn't you waste a lot of fruitless energy on account of most of them? Didn't most of them turn out to be all right after all?

Dale Carnegie

"God never built a Christian strong enough to carry today's duties and tomorrow's anxieties piled on top of them" (Theodore Ledyard Cuyler). The psalmist found the best way to combat fear: "But when I am afraid, I will put my confidence in you. Yes, I will trust the promises of God. And since I am trusting him, what can mere man do to me?" (Ps. 56:3–4 TLB).

Don't Postpone Joy

Enthusiasm makes everything different. You can't control the length of your life, but you can control its width and depth by adding fun and enthusiasm. When you have enthusiasm for life, life has enthusiasm for you. "He that is of a merry heart hath a continual feast" (Prov. 15:15). William Ward said, "Enthusiasm and persistence can make an average person superior; indifference and lethargy can make a superior person average."

"Always be joyful. Always keep on praying. No matter what happens, always be thankful, for this is God's will for you who belong to Christ Jesus" (1 Thess. 5:16–18 TLB). Don't postpone joy. Joy is the most infallible sign of the presence of God. It's the echo of God's life within us. Enthusiasm is an inside job.

A little girl walked to and from school each day. Though the weather one morning was questionable and clouds were forming, she made her daily trek to school. As the afternoon progressed, the winds whipped up, along with lightning. The mother of the little girl felt concerned that her daughter would be frightened as she walked home from school. She also feared the electrical storm might harm her child.

Full of concern, the mother got into her car and quickly drove along the route to her child's school. As she did, she saw her little girl walking along. At each flash of lightning, the child would stop, look up, and smile. More lightning followed quickly, and with each flash, the little girl would look at the streak of light and smile.

When the mother drew up beside the child, she lowered the window and called, "What are you doing?"

The child answered, "I am trying to look pretty because God keeps taking my picture."

Face the storms that come your way with a smile of hope.

Enthusiasm and pessimism are contagious. How much of each do you spread? You can succeed at almost anything for which you have unlimited enthusiasm. "It's difficult to remain neutral or indifferent in the presence of a positive thinker" (Denis Waitley).

One of the single most powerful things you can do to have influence over others is to smile at them. You're never fully dressed until you wear a smile. The best facelift is a smile. A smile is an asset; a frown is a liability. Some people grin and bear it; others smile and change it. "Be like the Mona Lisa. She keeps smiling when her back's to the wall" (Shelby Friedman).

"In my experience, the best creative work is never done when one is unhappy" (Albert Einstein). Every success of genius must be the result of enthusiasm. For every opportunity you miss because you're too enthusiastic, you will miss a hundred because you're not enthusiastic enough. I prefer the foolishness of enthusiasm to the indifference of logic.

If you find yourself dog-tired at night, it may be because you growled all day. Learn to laugh at yourself. A person with a great sense of humor may bore others, but he never has had a dull moment himself. "Of all the things God created, I am often most grateful He created laughter" (Chuck Swindoll). Humor is to life what shock absorbers are to automobiles.

You will rarely succeed at anything unless you have fun doing it.

God Will Use You Right Where You Are Today

Y ou don't need to do anything else for God to begin to use you now. You don't have to read another book, listen to another cassette tape, memorize another passage, plant another seed gift, or repeat another creed or confession. You don't even need to attend another church service before God can use you.

God uses willing vessels, not brimming vessels. Throughout the Bible, in order to fulfill His plans for the earth, God used all kinds of people from all walks of life:

- Matthew, a government employee who became an apostle
- Gideon, a common laborer who became a valiant leader of men

- Jacob, a deceiver and refugee whose name became Israel and who became the father of the twelve tribes of Israel
- Deborah, a housewife who became a judge
- Moses, a stutterer who became a deliverer
- Jeremiah, a child who fearlessly spoke the Word of the Lord
- Aaron, a servant who became God's spokesman
- Nicodemus, a Pharisee who became a defender of the faith
- David, a shepherd boy who became a king
- Hosea, a marital failure who prophesied to save Israel
- Joseph, a prisoner who became prime minister
- Esther, an orphan who became a queen
- Elijah, a homely man who became a mighty prophet

- Joshua, an assistant who became a conqueror
- James and John, fishermen who became close disciples of Christ and were known as the "sons of thunder"
- Abraham, a nomad who became the father of many nations
- John the Baptist, a vagabond who became the forerunner of Jesus
- Mary, an unknown virgin who gave birth to the Son of God
- Nehemiah, a cupbearer who built the wall of Jerusalem
- Shadrach, Meshach, and Abednego, Hebrew exiles who became great leaders in the Babylonian Empire
- Hezekiah, an idolatrous father's son, who became a king renowned for doing right in the sight of the Lord
- Isaiah, a man of unclean lips who prophesied the birth of God's Messiah

- Paul, a self-righteous persecutor who became the greatest missionary in history and the author of two-thirds of the books of the New Testament

All God needs is all of you!

Do You Count Your Blessings, or Do You Think Your Blessings Don't Count?

> If the only prayer you say in your whole life is "Thank you," that would suffice.
>
> Meister Eckhart

Do you have an attitude of gratitude? If we would stop to think more, we would stop to thank more. Of all the human feelings, gratitude has the shortest memory.

Cicero said, "A thankful heart is not only the greatest virtue, but the parent of all other virtues." The degree to which you are thankful is a sure index of your spiritual health. Max

Lucado wrote, "The devil doesn't have to steal anything from you, all he has to do is make you take it for granted." When you count all of your blessings, you will always show a profit.

Replace regret with gratitude. Be grateful for what you have, not regretful for what you don't have. If you can't be thankful for what you have, be thankful for what you have escaped. Henry Ward Beecher said, "The unthankful . . . discovers no mercies; but the thankful heart . . . will find in every hour, some heavenly blessings." The more you complain, the less you'll obtain.

> If we get everything we want, we will soon want nothing that we get.
>
> Vernon Luchies

If you don't enjoy what you have, how could you be happier with more? Francis Schaeffer said, "The beginning of men's rebellion against God was, and is, the lack of a thankful heart." The seeds of discouragement will not grow in a thankful heart. Erich Fromm remarked, "Greed is a bottomless pit which exhausts the person in an endless effort to satisfy the need without ever reaching satisfaction."

Epicurus reflected, "Nothing is enough for the man to whom enough is too little." It's a sure sign of mediocrity to be moderate with our thanks. Don't find yourself so busy asking God for favors that you have no time to thank Him. I relate to what Joel Budd said: "I feel like I'm the one who wrote *Amazing Grace*."

> Happiness always looks small while you hold it in your hands, but let it go, and you learn at once how big and precious it is.
>
> Maxim Gorky

I believe we should have the attitude of George Hubert, who said, "Thou, O Lord, has given so much to me, give me one more thing—a grateful heart." The Bible says (in Psalms), "Let us come before His presence with thanksgiving" (author's paraphrase). Our thanks to God should always precede our requests of Him. The Bible challenges us in 1 Thessalonians 5:17–18, "Pray without ceasing. In everything give thanks" (NKJV).

"We don't thank God for much he has given us. Our prayers are too often the beggar's prayer, the prayer that asks for something. We offer too few prayers of thanksgiving and of praise" (Robert Woods). Don't find yourself at the end of your life saying, "What a wonderful life I've had! I only wish I'd realized it and appreciated it sooner."

> Thank God for dirty dishes;
>   they have a tale to tell.
> While other folks go hungry,
>   we're eating pretty well.
> With home, and health, and
>   happiness,
>   we shouldn't want to fuss;
> For by this stack of evidence,
>   God's very good to us.
>
>   Anonymous

Never Let Yesterday Use Up Too Much of Today

Yesterday ended last night. So today it's more valuable to look ahead and prepare than to look back and regret. Don't let regrets replace your dreams. "A man is not old until regrets take the place of dreams" (John Barrymore). Regret looks back. Worry looks around. Faith looks up.

Life can be understood backward, but it must be lived forward. The past should be viewed with gratitude for the good things God has done, so look backward with gratitude and forward with confidence.

Your past is the start of your fresh start. Consider what Vivian Laramore said: "I've shut the door on yesterday and thrown the key away—tomorrow holds no fears for me, since I've found today." Use the past as a launching pad, not a lawn chair. Dreams of the future are more valuable than the history of the past. "The wise man looks ahead. The fool attempts to fool himself and won't face facts" (Prov. 14:8 TLB).

Experience is at best yesterday's answer to today's problem. It should only be a guide, not a jailer. Your past is not your potential. Never build your future around your past. The past is over. You must be willing to shed part of your previous life. If past history were all that mattered, librarians would be the most successful people in the world.

God doesn't review your past to determine your future. "Remember ye not the former things, neither consider the things of old. Behold, I will do a new thing; now it shall spring forth; shall ye not know it? I will even make a way in the wilderness, and rivers in the desert" (Isa. 43:18–19).

"Keep your eye on the road, and use your

rearview mirror only to avoid trouble" (Daniel Meacham). Stop taking journeys into the past. Don't make the mistake of letting yesterday use up too much of today.

John Mason is a national bestselling author, noted speaker, and executive author coach. He is the founder and president of Insight International, an organization dedicated to helping people reach their God-given dreams and fulfill their destinies.

He's authored twenty-eight books, including *Believe You Can*, *An Enemy Called Average*, *You're Born an Original—Don't Die a Copy*, and *Know Your Limits—Then Ignore Them*. His books have sold over two million copies and are translated into thirty-eight languages throughout the world. John's books are widely known as a source of godly wisdom, genuine motivation, and practical principles. Known for his quick wit, powerful thoughts, and insightful ideas, he's a popular speaker across the United States and around the world.

You can contact John Mason at:
contact@freshword.com
www. Freshword.com
918-493-1718

Find More Wisdom from
John Mason

freshword.com |

We need to stop asking,
WHY ME? and start asking,
WHAT NEXT?

With his signature infectious positive energy, John
Mason offers anyone looking for direction this simple
yet powerful message of encouragement and hope—
you can seize today and uncover a brighter tomorrow.
How? By asking the right questions to find the answers
for success and happiness.

 Revell
a division of Baker Publishing Group
www.RevellBooks.com

Everything you want
is on the other side of
NOT GIVING UP

In this inspiring book, Mason gives you fifty-two keys to never giving up on your dreams. He shows you how to move forward when you're on the verge of quitting, how to avoid unnecessary trouble, and how to keep your energy level up in the face of setbacks.

Revell
a division of Baker Publishing Group
www.RevellBooks.com

Available wherever books and ebooks are sold.